The Future of Money

From Financial Crisis to Public Resource

MARY MELLOR

PlutoPress
www.plutobooks.com

First published 2010 by Pluto Press
345 Archway Road, London N6 5AA and
175 Fifth Avenue, New York, NY 10010

www.plutobooks.com

Distributed in the United States of America exclusively by
Palgrave Macmillan, a division of St. Martin's Press LLC,
175 Fifth Avenue, New York, NY 10010

British Library Cataloguing in Publication Data
A catalogue record for this book is available from the British Library

ISBN   978 0 7453 2995 6   Hardback
ISBN   978 0 7453 2994 9   Paperback

Library of Congress Cataloging in Publication Data applied for

This book is printed on paper suitable for recycling and made from
fully managed and sustained forest sources. Logging, pulping and
manufacturing processes are expected to conform to the environmental
standards of the country of origin.

10   9   8   7   6   5   4   3   2   1

Designed and produced for Pluto Press by
Chase Publishing Services Ltd, 33 Livonia Road, Sidmouth, EX10 9JB, England
Typeset from disk by Stanford DTP Services, Northampton, England
Printed and bound in the European Union by
CPI Antony Rowe, Chippenham and Eastbourne

For Kate and Joe

CONTENTS

ACKNOWLEDGEMENTS

Many, many thanks to Molly Scott Cato, Paul Langley, Sue Bennet and Nigel Mellor for their careful reading of the text and very helpful comments and suggestions. Thanks also to Roger van Zwanenberg for helping frame the book and to two anonymous referees for very useful suggestions.

INTRODUCTION

The financial crisis of 2007–08 has revealed both the instability
of the global financial system and the importance of the state
as lender, borrower and investor of last resort. The world of
deregulated privatised finance proved not to be a source of wealth
for all, but a drain on the public economy, as states poured money
into the private financial sector. It has also been a destroyer of
personal economic security as savings were threatened, jobs lost
and homes repossessed. The crisis in the financial sector, most
notably in Britain and the United States, but also in Europe and
many other parts of the world, contrasts with the bombastic
optimism of the latter part of the twentieth century and the early
part of the twenty-first century with its glory days of 'Big Bang'
deregulation and the financial sector's dominance over national
politics. Far from celebrating the 'rolling back' of the 'nanny' state,
the implosion of deregulated finance has directly contradicted the
neoliberal case that the market and its money system is a self-
regulating process that will only be distorted by state intervention.
  The crisis raises many questions about the way the financial
system operates under late capitalism, in particular the role
of banks and other financial institutions. The financial system
is about the flow of money in its many forms through human
societies and this, in turn, raises questions about the nature of
money itself. Is money just a mechanism that represents economic
processes or is it a social mechanism in its own right? Where does
money come from, how does it operate? Who controls money, and
how? In this book the case will be made that money is a complex
phenomenon whose economic functioning relies on social trust
and public authority. The role of states in attempting to rescue
the financial sector challenges the idea that money is a purely
economic phenomenon. The crisis reveals money's social and

1

political base, but also its enormous power and lack of democratic control. It is therefore crucially important to understand how money operates within the capitalist market system and how the institutions that originate and direct its flow are owned and controlled. This book does not assume any prior knowledge of economics but will be of interest to those within the discipline who want to look beyond conventional economic analysis. For those seeking more radical approaches, it aims to broaden the debates about the crisis in the financial system in order to explore possible alternatives by looking at the wider social and political context of the financial crisis.

Capitalist market theory sees money as the representation and product of a 'wealth-creating' economic system. As such, its operation should be left as far as possible to market logic. The case for the 'free' market and the privatisation of the money system is that markets are the most efficient way to organise and distribute economic goods, including finance. Given the assumption that all wealth is created by the private sector, the public/social sector is seen as parasitic upon this money/wealth creation process. Money circulation through the financial system is seen as the outcome of private economic acts, not as a function of social relationships and public authority. The notion that money issue and circulation should reflect the demands of the market means that public expenditure must always be contingent on the activities of private economic actors. Expenditure on social or public needs must be secondary to privatised economic forces. The private sector will authorise how much can, or cannot, be afforded since public expenditure is seen as a drain upon the private sector.

The financial collapse has exposed the neoliberal ideology of market fundamentalism for the illusion it always was. In capitalist economies, the state is a capitalist state and has always stood behind the capitalist financial system as guardian of the money system, financial properties and contracts. Although public sector spending is decried, the state is expected to produce unlimited sums of money to stabilise the financial system when it experiences its regular crises. The exposure of the reliance of the private financial sector on the state has brought the financial system into full view and opens it up for analysis. The opportunity must be taken to challenge the private control of finance and ask whether such an important aspect of human society should be owned by, and serve, the interests of capitalism. If the conventional view of money and its systems is not challenged, public intervention in the financial sector during the current crisis will only be a stepping stone back to hidden state support of a more carefully regulated capitalist financial sector – until the next crisis.

The core argument of this book is that the money system needs to be reclaimed from the profit-driven market economy and socially administered for the benefit of society as a whole as a public resource. In order to make this case it is important to look in detail at the nature, history and functioning of money and its institutions. There are dilemmas in opening up a debate about the nature of money and its role in economic life. The ideology of the market presents the economy as a natural process administered by inspired entrepreneurs in which exchange through money is conducted on rational principles. To say that money is as much a social and political phenomenon as an economic one is not an easy case to make. Confidence in money has largely been based on illusions about the origins of money and how it is issued and circulated. Will people be able to live within a financial system that operates without those illusions?

Modern societies are heavily monetised so that nearly all human needs are met through monetary exchange, whether in direct purchases or through taxation and state expenditure. Many people also try to secure their future through money: in savings, pensions or other financial assets. It is therefore important that people feel that money is a tangible thing that has value and will hold that value. People must trust money and trust other people to hold to their money contracts if they are to feel secure. They must feel that their money is safe in the bank, that their pension will be paid or that the price of bread will be within their means. The case this book will make is that this economic security can only be achieved through public action and social solidarity, not through the market. In this context it is important to challenge the concept of the market itself. The capitalist market is not created to meet needs, it is created to make profit.

As radical economists, from Marxists to greens and feminists, have argued, the capitalist market system presents itself as a 'natural' system while distorting human societies and destroying ecological systems. Feminist and green economists, in particular, have argued that the money system draws artificial boundaries around economic valuation that excludes women's unpaid work and ecological damage. A more comprehensive concept of the economy that describes the meeting of human need both inside and outside of the money system is provisioning. In order to live fulfilling lives people need a wide range of supportive relationships and secure access to sustenance. They need physical goods and services, but they also need many other things including care and friendship, time and space to develop their skills and personality. Some of these are provided by the money economy (public and private) but many are not. Many of these needs are denied through pressure of work and lack of resources, including money. Some are achieved only through great personal sacrifice. One of the aims of this book is to explore whether it is possible to have a money system that could enable a comprehensive provisioning of human societies in an ecologically sustainable and socially just way. Understanding the present money system is central to achieving that end.

The first chapter will explore the origin, nature and function of money. It will look at different ways that money has been construed: as private, related to the capitalist market; as public, related to the authority of the state or as social, a construct of social relationships and trust. Concepts will be explored such as 'sound' money and the relation of money to the 'real' economy. The chapter will look at the way that control of money has shifted over time from public authority to the privatised banking system. It will be argued that this shift is important because ownership and control of the issue and circulation of money gives to the issuer the benefit of initial expenditure of that money and, with that, direction of the economy as a whole.

The privatisation of money issue and circulation will be explored further in the second chapter which will look at the ownership and control of the financial system institutions. It will show how money issue and circulation has moved between the private and public sector in an intricate relationship between the state, commerce and the banking sector. It will show how government reliance on debt to the private sector was central to the modern banking system. This has been amplified by the shift from state issue of debt free money, mainly as notes and coin, to private bank generated debt-based money, which is effectively 'fresh air money' or 'money from nowhere'. The radical implications of this will be explored. The chapter will go on to look at the changes that took place in banking in the late twentieth century which saw an explosion of new financial instruments and financial institutions. These innovations in the financial system, together with the globalisation of finance and a political regime of light regulation, laid the basis for the 2007–08 financial crisis.

The third chapter will argue that the privatisation of money issue and circulation has led to the emergence of a financialised society where money value predominates. This has undermined public and collective approaches to social solidarity and security, particularly within the Anglo-American economies. Concepts such as 'people's capitalism' and 'the property owning democracy' have encouraged people to think that they can individually safeguard their interests through the money system. As a result, public and collective assets have been privatised or demutualised and people have been encouraged to become shareholders, rather than members and citizens. The chapter will explore how people were enticed into financial capitalism through pensions, stock market investments and, particularly, mortgages. Savings became confused with investment with little awareness of risk. In the short term the stock market and house prices boomed. Personal credit also exploded as a major engine of capitalist expansion. Easy access to credit masked stagnant levels of pay. The use of credit also became central to policy responses to social need, poverty and inequality. Strategies such as microcredit saw people, particularly women, encouraged to borrow and invest their way out of poverty. While debt had seemingly been democratised, the foundations were being laid for the future credit crisis.

Chapter four looks at the main beneficiaries of the massive issue and circulation of credit under the privatised financial system. In the late twentieth century the financial sector eclipsed the productive sector of the Anglo-American economies and captured the policy agenda. Speculative investment appeared to be a crock of gold that promised capital gains for everyone, from the personal investor to the house owner and the pensioner. The chapter will explore the way in which debt became a major resource for speculative financial investment both in terms of 'leverage', that is, debt based speculation, and debt related 'derivatives' such as debts sold on as investments or insurance on debt. New forms of investment organisations fuelled by debt appeared, such as private equity companies and hedge funds. Public assets were sold off and public investment was privatised through private finance initiatives. The chapter will explore the implications of this latest phase of speculative finance capitalism and its role in creating the conditions for the financial crisis.

The fifth chapter will describe the key stages of the financial crisis as it moved from the trigger of a subprime crisis to a banking and financial crisis and finally to a full-blown economic crisis. The origins of the crisis will be traced to the changes in banking and personal finance as described in chapters two and three and the activities of speculative finance capitalism explained in chapter four. It will be argued that what the crisis clearly reveals is the public underpinning of the financial sector, as states across the world struggle to sustain their banking systems, and increasingly the wider financial sector, through 'Wall Street Socialism'.

The sixth chapter will look at the underlying causes and implications of the financial crisis. It will ask whether any lessons have been learned, or if the expectation is that everything will return to business as usual. It will be argued that the analysis of money and banking in chapters one and two shows that the privatisation of the money system has been built upon false assumptions. The immediacy and intensity of the financial crisis has exposed the illusion of prosperity through finance capitalism and the fragility of market oriented financial systems. While private ownership and control of the creation and circulation of money has been vital to the dynamics of capitalism, it has ultimately rested on public and social foundations. The case will be made for seeing money as a socially constructed and publicly authorised resource that should be subject to democratic control.

The last chapter will look at ways in which money as a public resource could enable complex societies to meet their needs without the exploitation of each other, other societies or the natural environment. A 'sufficiency' or 'steady-state' means of provisioning would require a money system that could maintain circulation without demanding unnecessary growth. This would meet green demands that any provisioning system should be ecologically sustainable and the feminist argument that it should recognise all forms of beneficial work and activities. The chapter will look at a range of proposals for how the money and banking system could be reformed in order to provide a practical financial basis for a democratic, ecologically sustainable and socially just provisioning system.

Capitalism has survived many other credit-led booms, growth reversals and fraudulent episodes; is this just another of capitalism's many crises or a crisis that may undermine its hegemony sufficiently both to enable and demand radical alternatives at the national and global level? The failure of the Anglo-American attempt to financialise society and turn the whole population into investors has shown that the idea of the democratisation of financial capitalism is a contradiction in terms. The huge cost of the financial implosion and its impact on the productive economy has fractured the dogma of the privatised money system and the supremacy of the capitalist market. Privatised control of the money system has meant that the benefits of the money system have been privatised while the risks have been socialised. Will the fact that so many people have been touched by capitalism's failure this time spell its demise? Will it open up space for more socially just and ecologically sustainable alternatives to emerge? In order to open this debate it is important to discuss money itself.

1

WHAT IS MONEY?

This is not a straightforward question. Money in its long history has been represented by many different things from precious metals, shells and beads to heavy, largely unmoveable stones. It has been made of substances that have value in themselves such as precious metals or represented by something that has no value in itself such as base metal coin or paper. Its operation has been represented in many ways from cuneiform tablets and tally sticks, to paper or electronic records. Conventional economics sees money as having a number of functions. It is a measure of value (a unit of account), a medium of exchange, a way of making deferred payments and a store of value. Money is seen as evolving with the market system. Barter is often assumed to be the original form of economic exchange with money emerging to solve the problem of finding suitable mutual exchanges. From this perspective, money is the product of pre-existing economic exchange.

The chosen commodity needed to be valuable, durable, divisible and portable. Precious metals such as gold and silver were obvious choices. As a result, gold has been particularly resonant for modern conceptions of money. Gold is seen as having an inherent or intrinsic value and was adopted as a basis for money value until comparatively recently. From this 'metallist' perspective, the value of money still relates back to gold or some commodity that has intrinsic value although, in practice, money can be represented in many forms, such as base metal coin, paper or electronic record. This view of money leads to the assumption that money can only function effectively if it is scarce and valuable. Douthwaite argues that this view, based on the historical scarcity of gold and silver, has distorted economic theory ever since. It has led to the false idea that money can only be based on a scarce, and therefore valued, resource (1999:33).

The claim that money originated in barter has also been challenged (Innes 1913/2004, Ingham 2004, Smithin 2009). Rather than tying the origins of money directly to the emergence of a market economy, a variety of early uses have been identified such as tribute, *wergeld* (injury payment) or temple money (offerings). Money has also appeared in many different types of society and in many different forms. The emphasis on street level portable money in western economic thinking may reflect the fact that in Europe coin emerged a thousand years before banking. However, in historical terms the banking function is thousands of years older still. It emerged in Ancient Egypt and Babylon which both had extensive banking functions based upon grain storage. The invention of money as coin is credited to the Lydians of Greek Asia Minor in the seventh century BCE who made coin out of electrum, a naturally occurring gold/silver alloy. Alexander the Great (356–323 BCE) minted coins to fund his military campaigns and expand his empire. The Romans also used coins widely and their value was set on the authority of Rome. After the fall of Rome the use of coin became more chaotic in Europe and was even abandoned in Britain. However by the seventh and eighth centuries coins were circulating through much of Asia, the Middle East and Europe. Some of these coins travelled long distances, particularly the *denier*, a silver coin (Spufford 1988:40). Even so, as Buchan notes, until the twelfth century gold and silver were as likely to be used for decoration as money. However, from the twelfth century onwards the balance between decorative uses and money shifted in the direction of money and religious artefacts were being melted down and minted into coin to fund the crusades (Buchan 1997:53).

Although coins have historically been associated with precious metal such as silver and gold, as Mitchell Innes pointed out as early as 1913, the amount of precious metal in coin has varied widely over time. Rarely has the value of the actual coin been the same as the value of the metal of which it is made (Innes 1913/2004). Given the varying amount of precious metal in coins, the only guarantee of the worth of the coin became the face or signature of the issuer, basically the authority behind the minting. Far from being a precious commodity that had become readily accepted through trade as the barter theorists thought, money as coin has generally been issued by fiat, that is, issued and guaranteed by an authority, such as a powerful leader, an office-holder or a religious organisation. In fact, as Davies has argued, when coins were too closely associated with scarce precious metal, economic activities became restricted. Economies flourished where coins were plentiful, such that 'long run trends in depression and prosperity correlate extremely well with the precious metal famine and surplus of the Middle Ages' (Davies 2002:646). Even debasing the coinage by reducing the precious metal content was not in itself a problem as the countries which experienced the greatest economic growth were those whose leaders had 'indulged in the most severe debasement' of their coinage (Davies 2002:647).

Making coin out of a precious metal confuses the role of money as a measure of value with the value of the coin itself. Since gold and silver have value as commodities, it would seem reasonable to imagine that their value is intrinsic to the coins themselves. However to say that silver and gold have intrinsic value is not the same as saying that a gold coin has a particular value, certainly not one that is constant over time. Gold can change value both as a commodity and as a coin in terms of purchasing power. Therefore gold/silver as a commodity does not 'have' a value. It is valued, but at any point in time the exact value will vary and will need to be designated in some other form of commodity or money, such as silver or dollars. As Rossi argues, money cannot be a commodity because its value would need to be established using another standard of value such that 'infinite recursivity makes this measurement logically impossible' (2007:13). Money value is therefore much less certain than even an arbitrary measure such as an inch. Once an inch is chosen as a unit of measurement it stays constant, whereas money as a unit of measurement can never be assumed to be constant no matter what it is made of. Money does not in itself embody a value, it measures relative values.

The historical popularity of scarce metal has obscured the fact that to say that something is worth a few shavings of silver, an electronic money sum, a number of gold coins, wampum beads or a Yap stone is all the same thing, that is, different ways of measuring value. The Yap stones of Yap in Micronesia are particularly interesting as they are large stones that can only be moved with great difficulty, if at all. Value does not imply anything about the material from which money is made. Gold and silver are therefore valued for themselves, but cannot act as a fixed measure of value, nor can they secure the value of a currency. Despite some contemporary arguments that money should be returned to a connection with precious metal (Lewis 2007:409), money is more helpfully seen not as a 'thing' but as a social form (Ingham 2004:80). Ingham sees the idea that there is some 'invariant monetary standard' as a 'working fiction' (2004:144). 'Sound money' is a product of society, not of nature. Money is something that people trust to maintain its value or be honoured in trade, while its actual value can vary. Effectively when we say people trust in money we mean they are trusting in the organisations, society and authorities that create and circulate it, other people, traders, the banks and the state. Money, whatever its form, is a social construction, not a natural form. It has no inherent value but it has vast social and political power (Hutchinson et al. 2002:211).

This insight has not always been clear in radical thought. Marx, for example, was close to the ideas of the commodity theorists on the origins of money. At the same time, he saw the money relation as a social relation. This makes confusing reading. Marx seems at times to say that money is based on valuable metal and at other times that money has no value (Mellor 2005:50). He adopts a commodity theory of money as 'a single commodity set aside for that purpose' (Marx 1867/1954:36). However that commodity must be socially identified: 'a particular commodity cannot become the universal equivalent except by a social act... thus it becomes – money' (Marx 1954:58); 'money itself has no price' (Marx 1954:67), and the even more confusing, 'although gold and silver are not by nature money, money is by nature gold and silver' (Marx 1954:61). This is mainly because Marx's focus isn't money itself, but the exploited labour embodied in the exchange process that is obscured by the money system: 'When arose the illusions of the monetary system? To it gold and silver when serving as money did not represent a social relation between producers, but were natural objects with strange properties' (Marx 1954:54). One result of Marx's confusing statements and the focus on the labour theory of value is that the analysis of money has not been central to radical economic thought. In this sense, much radical and conventional economic theorising shares a common idea that money is only the representation of a 'real economy' of economic exchange and is therefore of no special interest within economic theorising.

As we have seen, coins confuse the analysis of money if they are made of something that has a separate value as a commodity. This is not the case with paper money. Paper itself cannot have any inherent value as a substance. Whatever it represents must be the basis of a social agreement. Like coin, paper money has a long history. It was first used in ninth-century China during the Hein Tsung period 806–821 and the paper money of the empire of Kubla Khan (1260–1294) was recognised from China to the Baltic. Within Europe paper-based exchange was vital to the growth of commercial markets. Trade was enabled through promissory notes (based on the personal trustworthiness of the issuer) and bills of exchange (linked to the sale of goods) issued by traders and goldsmiths. Paper money also avoided more risky forms of payment such as carrying gold or coin. The exchange of paper was supported by the development of double entry book-keeping that was widely used in trading cities such as Genoa by the mid-fourteenth century. The use of paper money and book-keeping systems enabled an expansion of trade that was free of the limitation of precious metal.

However this does not necessarily undermine the commodity theory of money. Paper money can be seen as merely representing, and being backed by, the original precious metal. The notion that there was a precious metal reserve 'backing' currencies was retained until the early 1970s through the attachment of currencies to a dollar value for gold. This did not claim that there was an inherent value in gold, but that currency values should be based on the nominal value of gold priced in dollars. However, any real backing of currencies by gold would be impossible in modern economies (or even many traditional economies) given its scarcity: 'the very notion of a commodity money is an illusion' (Parguez and Seccareccia 2000:106). The dollar maintained this fiction the longest and it was the strain on American gold reserves that led to the final abolition of any attachment to gold in the early 1970s. On coming to power in 1997 the UK Chancellor of the Exchequer, Gordon Brown, acknowledged the impracticality of gold as a currency reserve by selling half the country's reserves and buying instead a range of currencies: dollars, yen and euros. The alternative to the 'metallist' or commodity theory of money is a theory that sees money as resting on a social and political base, a combination of social conventions, banking systems and state authority.

Money as a Social Phenomenon

The theory of the barter economy saw money as emerging organically out of the market. Ingham argues that this is logically impossible as the market could not exist without money and therefore 'money is logically anterior and historically prior to market exchange' (2004:25). Ingham makes this argument because he focuses on a different aspect of money from the barter theorists. The latter stress the importance of money as a medium of exchange, with the chosen valuable commodity taking the place of bartered goods. For Ingham, the most important aspect of money is its use as a notional or abstract measure of value which he sees as preceding coin by 2,000–3,000 years (Ingham 2004:12). Even barter would need to have a notional scale of values with which to measure a carrot against a cabbage. For Ingham, measuring value in economic exchange is much more important than the actual medium used to transfer value. This is why the large and immoveable Yap stone can act as money if people calculate value in relation to it. The British guinea (21 shillings, or 105p) existed as a measure of value for a long time after the coin ceased to exist.

Money as currency is therefore not valuable because of its metal or other physical content as the metallist commodity theory of money claims, rather, it is a token of value. The latter 'Chartalist' approach (Chartal is taken from the Latin for token) sees the value of money as resting on the power of the issuer, not the intrinsic worth of the money. From the social perspective, whatever form money takes, that form does not embody a real value in itself. It is a token representing a notional value that is universally accepted and can be readily transferred. Money's value therefore is not 'natural', it is not determined by its metallic content or backing, nor does it emerge naturally from market relations. It is socially constructed. Whatever form it takes, what matters is that people agree to honour the value it represents. As Dodd argues, 'money depends for its existence and circulation in society on a generalised level of trust in its abstract properties' (1994:160).

For social theories of money the actual money-stuff that represents the accounting process is not important as long as people trust it. Whatever value money is given, it represents a credit or claim on the future production of society. Rather than being secured by some inherent value of the money-stuff itself, the social theory of money sees it as 'a socially (including politically) constructed promise...money is always an abstract claim or credit' (Ingham 2004:198). For Ingham 'moneyness' is provided by whatever is agreed as the 'money of account', that is the means of calculating the relative value of goods, services, debts or taxes. Holding money is a claim on society and all money is therefore a credit that can command resources based on whatever value it carries at any point in time (Wray 2004:234). The social view of money sees it as a system of credit-debt relations that is socially created and maintained. Money is a credit for those who hold it as it is a claim on future consumption or investment. At the same time it is a debt on those who have to provide the goods or services demanded when the holders present their money. They must give up a service or a product for what is effectively a credit note: 'All money is debt in so far as issuers promise to accept their own money for *any* debt payment by *any* bearer of money' (Ingham 2004:198 [italics in the original]). For money to function effectively, whoever circulates money tokens in society must honour them by accepting them in payment, or guarantee them as a means of access to goods and services.

While the money system can be seen as a network of claims and obligations, for money to be universally acceptable it has to be given social credibility through respected authorities or institutions. Socially constructed money can emerge in many contexts, but modern money was built from an intricate relationship between the emerging capitalist market and the state (Knapp 1924, Ingham 2004, Wray 2004, Smithin 2009). Power holders issued coin that had notional value and uncertain metal content, but even where gold and silver were in good supply, paper money formed the basis of many commercial transactions (Spufford 1988:259). Paper records of trades (bills of exchange) and credit (promissory notes or bonds) were used widely, particularly in the early north Italian trading cities (Ferguson 2008:41). The important shift came when this commercial paper became transferable, that is, when it did not just represent an agreement between people who knew and trusted each other, but could pass from hand to hand. Commercial paper became money when it was not tied to a particular credit-debt relationship of traders who knew each other, but could be used by any bearer for any purpose. For this to happen, money must achieve a high level of general trust, which rests on a stable social structure of authority such as well-established governments, traders or banks. As Zelizer has argued, 'money was not the automatic, irrepressible outcome of...market economies...the creation of a centralized, homogenous uniform legal tender took enormous and sustained effort' (Zelizer 1994:205). Smithin agrees that 'the monetary order is socially constructed, rather than deriving automatically from the market' (2009:70–1).

Modern banking, which brought together financial and political power, emerged in medieval Italy and led to the establishment of major banking dynasties such as the Medici. The early Italian banks issued loans far and wide, including to English kings (Ferguson 2008:41). Banks, named after the benches on which

the goldsmiths sat on the Rialto bridge in Venice, were vital
to developing modern money. Banks guaranteed payments by
issuing their own paper money or 'promise to pay' in place of
the commercial paper issued by traders or bonds (based on future
revenues). Such paper notes from trusted bankers circulated like
the coin issued by states. Notionally, behind the paper money
were the reserves of precious metal held by the banker, but the
real basis was a trust that all future payments would be made,
that is, that everyone would honour their obligations so that the
circulation of the trusted tokens could continue in perpetuity. As
will be explained more fully in the next chapter, contemporary
banking continues the link between commercial finance and
state authority.

Money can only exist within a 'monetary space', that is, one
where whatever is used as the 'money of account' in Ingham's
terms, is backed by an authority or a code of honour of some form
(Ingham 2004:140). Money that achieves value through authority
is described as fiat money. Fiat money is issued by authorities
who have the political or social capacity to make demands upon
others, as when monarchs issued coins. For Rossi, 'fiat money is
a form of credit that its issuer asks for, and obtains, from those
agents giving up goods and services in exchange for it' (2007:18).
However, the power to issue fiat coins or notes is not unlimited,
as their future value still has to be trusted by the population. The
demands on goods and services made by the issuer cannot be
more than the productive capacity of the population can stand.
The money system therefore rests on a combination of authority,
social trust and economic capacity (public or private).

The State and Money

Ingham argues that the state was central to the development of
modern money. Until private credit money was incorporated into
the fiscal system of states which provided a secure jurisdiction
and legitimacy, it remained 'in evolutionary terms, a dead-end'
(Ingham 2004:122). The state theory of money was set out by
Georg Knapp in the early 1900s. Central to his ideas was a link

between the issue and circulation of token money and state taxation. Rather than demanding goods and services directly, the state demands tax payment in a money that it designates. As Wray points out:

> ...what Knapp called the state money stage begins when the state chooses the unit of account and names the thing that it accepts in payment of obligation to itself – at the nominal value it assigns to the thing. The final step occurs when the state actually issues the money things it accepts. (2004:243)

In the case of coin, states have historically issued it as the 'money thing'. The state then demands taxes which have to be paid in the money it has already issued and spent. The money is then returned via taxes to be issued again and again. The authority of the state rests ultimately on its ability to tax back, and therefore re-circulate, its money. An important benefit of issuing the 'money thing' is that states have the benefit of 'seigniorage', that is, the first use of the money issued less the cost of producing it (Huber and Robertson 2000:8). How this money is spent depends on the nature of the state: whether it is for war, palaces, cathedrals, irrigation systems or other more mundane goods and services. Seigniorage is a major benefit of the ownership and control of money.

An important stage in the development of modern money was when the two forms of money, trade-issued credit and fiat money, were brought together. This occurred when the state declared that not only was its own fiat-issued money legal tender, but also bank notes issued in the process of trade. Legal tender means that the state will accept a designated form of money in payment of taxes and the state also demands that everyone else has to honour that form of money when it is presented as payment for goods or debts. In the contemporary money system, state authorised money is seen as 'high-powered money' (Ingham 2004:202). High-powered money represents such a high level of trust that it has the capacity ultimately to settle all debts. It is the money of final payment within the money system. Under the commodity or metallist theory of money the basis of this high-powered money was a store of precious metal. In practice, for both social and more market oriented theories, the basis of high-powered money is the capacity of the state to raise taxes and, behind that, the productive capacity of the national economy. For Victoria Chick money in the modern western economy rests on 'the mutuality of state and social support' (1992:142).

The public role of governments is to use their authority over the money system to secure the status of their money both nationally and internationally. States cannot always do this, as the collapse of the national currency in countries such as Zimbabwe shows. It is also difficult for states to guarantee financial commitments beyond their currency regime, particularly if those commitments outstrip the value of the national economy. There are also problems if another currency intrudes into the national money space, destabilising national currencies and undermining state control. Argentina in 2001–02, despite being a rich country in terms of resources, could not secure its currency because much of its population held their money in dollars. This, together with a very large informal economy (20–30 per cent), meant the Argentine state could not guarantee its tax income and so could not maintain viable high-powered money (Krugman 2008:38–41). As will be described in the next chapter, the private banking system has been central to the issue and circulation of money in modern economies and this has obscured the important role of the state in ensuring that money is 'sound'.

Money, Society and the 'Real Economy'

For commodity 'metallist' theorists of money, money emerges from the market economy of production and exchange. It is merely a reflection of the 'real economy' of production and exchange. However, the idea that the quantity of money should reflect the value of the activities of the economy does not sit very well with the idea of money being represented by something that the market cannot determine, that is, the amount of precious metal available. Conventional economics has, therefore, been more flexible in its attitude toward the ultimate basis of money. It does, however, still argue that the money system should reflect the needs of the market and therefore should be controlled by market forces. From this market-oriented perspective, the state, despite historically being a major force in money creation and circulation, should not interfere with the operation of the financial or commodity markets. The state should not be involved in the creation of money or, as far as possible, the spending of it.

Marxist theory agrees with conventional economic theory that money is only a representation of real economic relations. However, from a Marxist perspective, far from emerging benignly from market systems, the evolution of the money society has been a far from natural process (Wood 1999:7, Hutchinson et al. 2002:74). Money systems as represented in rents, taxes and waged labour have been imposed on people who have been from subsistence communities and who have been forced off the land. As economies became monetised, peasant populations were forced to sell their labour as lands were enclosed and privatised, and often mortgaged (Rowbotham 1998:31). For those without land, joining the money economy meant obtaining sustenance through waged labour. Spufford (1988:245) argues that the circulation and use of coin from the early middle ages enabled rich landowners to extract more flexible wealth from their feudal populations. Rather than extracting produce or labour, they began to demand money from their peasant populations. There were limits to the benefits that could be obtained from exploiting peasant labour directly or receiving a portion of their produce, but payment in money opened the possibility of wider consumption of luxury goods. Landlords could use their money wealth to become more urbanised and absentee, enjoying the benefits of city life (Veblen 1899). Money systems also enabled the emergence of finance capital which enhanced exploitation and the extraction of profit (Hilferding 1910/1985).

Marx argued that profit-driven, money-based exchange distorted the nature of human activities. People did not labour to produce what they needed, but what could be commodified, that is sold for money:

this division of a product into a useful thing and a value becomes practically important only when exchange has acquired such an extension that useful articles are produced for the purpose of being exchanged and their character as value has therefore been taken into account beforehand during production. (Marx 1867/1954:44)

Marx made a distinction between producing a good and then selling it in order to buy another commodity, that is, when a commodity (C) is exchanged for money (M) and is then exchanged for another commodity (C) expressed as C – M – C. Full commodification comes when the intention of production, rather than the utility of the product itself, is to make money. Money is invested to produce a commodity which is sold to earn more money, expressed as M – C – M+. At this point, 'exchange values…do not contain an atom of use-value' (1954:4). The money value of the commodity exchanged is an expression of market forces and bears no relation to any intrinsic value of the commodity being exchanged.

In this process, those who labour have lost any control over the things they produce. They cannot choose what to produce as this is determined by those who pay for their labour. As people who have to work for a wage, they have already lost control of any means of subsistence they may once have had. Given the aim is to make a profit, the wages paid are less than the value of the product their labour produces and therefore the labourers are also ultimately unable to buy back the full value of what they produce. This creates a dilemma for capitalism in that it makes money by paying labour less than the full market value of their work, but if workers do not receive sufficient wages they cannot buy the products made. In the absence of an alternative market this means the seller's profit cannot be monetised, that is, turned into a readily transferable form. The huge surge in debt in western economies is one way in which this gap has been temporarily bridged. Equally, the need to find alternative markets was a major driver for western imperialism.

At the turn of the twentieth century, Georg Simmel put forward a more ambivalent view of the impact of money on society. He agreed that money rationalised social relations into 'the purest and most developed kind of interaction' (Simmel 1907/1970:82) which had the effect of alienating all other social values and led to social fragmentation. People became caught up in a process where 'the abstract value of wealth...represented by money is...the soul and purpose of economic activities' (Simmel 1907/1970:511). However, money payment was also 'the form most congruent with personal freedom' (1907/1970:285). Contemporary views of money reflect this ambivalence. Money-based societies are open in the sense that social status and traditional authority becomes less important than money wealth. However, money-based societies are more economically unequal as money is unevenly spread. Money is freedom in that 'money's empowerment of its holder derives from the freedom it provides for the expression of needs and desires' (Dodd 1994:159). At the same time 'money has been bound up with the unequal distribution of wealth and property whenever and wherever it has been found' (Dodd 1994:150). This is because money can be an instrument of speculation and a tool of empire (Lietaer 2001:332–3).

Viviana Zelizer, in a more social analysis of money, sees it as playing a different role in different sectors of society (1994:30). Money is certainly used in commodified exchange through the market, but it can also be used for other purposes such as a personal or charitable gift. It can signify a neutral business transaction or a personal relationship. Zelizer argues that money need not necessarily commodify, it is not always in opposition to community or solidarity and could lubricate social relations or enable the formation of an economic community (1994:211). While conventional economics and much of Marxist theory sees money as being a reflection of the 'real economy' of production and exchange, social analyses of money see it as being a phenomenon that has its own political dynamics (Hutchinson et al. 2002:24). As Smithin points out, the dominance of economic theorising based on the notion of barter exchange of goods and services remains virtually unchallenged within the economics literature, resulting in very little attention being paid to more social and political questions around the accumulation of financial resources (2009:9). Ingham sees the dominance of this apparently 'neutral' economic view of money as resulting from the fragmentation of the social sciences in the nineteenth century. Economics became separated from the other social sciences which meant that social and political questions about the nature of money were not posed (2004:197). Instead, conventional economic notions of money saw it as 'neutral' emerging organically from a 'natural' market system. In contrast Ingham argues that 'money cannot be neutral; it is the most powerful of the social technologies' (2004:202).

Not all economists marginalised the study of money: most notably Keynes saw money as a much more independent force. For Keynes 'money plays a part of its own and affects motives and decisions...we live...in a monetary economy' (Smithin 2009:60). Central to Keynes' ideas was the severe impact on the productive economy if the money system malfunctioned. Markets were not necessarily efficient and money might not circulate: money could be created but people might not spend it. The government might therefore need to intervene to maintain the circulation of money (that is, liquidity), so that effective demand continued within the economy (that is, demand backed by money) (Chick 2000). The recent financial crisis has certainly revealed how the productive economy is dependent on the functioning of the money system. The argument of this book is that as money is such a critical force in the circulation of goods and services and therefore provisioning, it is vital to question how money is issued and circulated, owned and controlled. From this perspective money is more than just a reflection of value in the 'real' economy.

Profit-oriented money-based market systems have brought condemnation from a range of social theorists and political activists. Religious institutions have expressed concern about lending money at interest and the danger of avarice, the love of money. Green economists see growth oriented and profit driven economies as destroying ecological systems because they do not recognise the way they damage and exploit natural resources (Scott Cato 2009:38). Instead such damage is financially 'externalised', meaning that economic calculations do not take account of these costs, treating the natural environment as a free resource. Ecofeminists combine the green critique with further criticism of the so-called 'real' economy: that it excludes the huge range of human activities associated with the work and lives of women that lie beyond the market (Mellor 1997). They claim that what economists study represents only a small part of humanity's existence in nature. The so-called 'real economy' is in reality an economy determined by capitalism and by patriarchy. Outside its boundaries lie the natural world and the un-monetised labour and needs of women, children and the poor, as well as non-monetised subsistence economies (Hutchinson et al. 2002:180, Bennholdt Thomsen and Mies 1999:19).

From this perspective it is a major error to confuse money-based exchange systems with 'the economy'. The monetised economy, by definition, covers only those things that are exchanged for money. Money puts a restrictive boundary around access to the means of sustenance. Private money-based ownership, together with property rights over resources and productive capacity, means that the money economy excludes or marginalises those without money. The money economy represents the priorities of those who have historically controlled the designation of certain human needs and activities as worthy of money payment. The money designated economy has been created through the priorities of dominant social groups, capitalist traders and higher waged workers, nearly all men. The patriarchal and capitalist market, therefore, cannot be seen as the source of value in a human society. It is not a neutral 'economic' choice to give something a monetary value, it is in essence a social and political choice that dominant groups and classes have imposed. To the extent that the public sector shares the same priorities as the market it, too, marginalises women and the natural world.

Instead of the narrow boundaries of 'the economy' presented in conventional economics, the wider notion of provisioning would cover all the goods and services human beings need to attain their full potential, as well as taking into account all the impacts they have on society and the environment: domestic life, social and neighbourly activities, activities for leisure and pleasure and the integrity of the environment (Power 2004:6). Failing to understand the social nature of money and how money is created leads to the environmentally ludicrous situation where activities for social or environmental benefit are rejected as 'unaffordable', while sports utility vehicles are produced in their millions, even in the face of peak oil. Such illogical activities in the name of 'the economy' have been described by Hazel Henderson as 'flat earth' economics (1981:21) and by Maria Mies and Vandana Shiva as 'mal-development' (1993:284).

Money: From Credit to Debt

The social theory of money argues that all money, whatever its form, is credit to the holder and a debt on society. Whatever form money takes it gives the holder the potential to purchase goods and services. The word credit comes from the Latin *credere*, to believe. The holder of money believes that it has value and so does the person who accepts it in payment. However, in contemporary usage, very confusingly, when we talk about credit we take this to mean debt. This is because the main way of issuing new money in contemporary society is through taking on debt. When an authority issued money by fiat it was debt free, apart from the cost of producing the coins or notes. In contemporary society when someone is 'given credit' this actually means she or he takes on a debt. Debt comes from the Latin word meaning to owe (*debere*).

All sectors of current society are involved in debt: the government, industry, households, individuals, the financial sector. Governments have historically borrowed to finance their activities from wars to social services; commercial traders and industrial producers have borrowed to finance their businesses; households have borrowed to finance home ownership; people have borrowed to buy consumer goods; recently in Britain and elsewhere this has been joined by student loans. In earlier eras economic activity was led by agricultural and industrial borrowing. Through much of the twentieth century, mortgage debt was an important sector for money issue in the US and the UK as the same houses were bought over and over again at ever increasing prices. In the early years of the twenty-first century, mortgage and personal debt expanded rapidly as did borrowing for financial speculation, fuelling the housing boom and leading to the credit crunch.

A fundamental problem of debt-based money issue is that it creates a growth imperative within the economy. People must find work of any sort, not only to meet current expenses but also to service their debts. Debt has long been used as a means of trapping people into work as in indentured labour. As well as its social impact, debt-driven labour can have ecological implications if people have to work unnecessarily hard or long, or engage in ecologically destructive patterns of production and consumption. As debts are paid with interest, the economy as a whole has to expand not only to cover the debt but the interest as well. Consequently there is a need for an ever expanding increase in debt-based money as more money must be paid back than was originally issued. In the short term this can be accounted for by faster circulation of the existing money form, but in the system as a whole there must be a source of expansion that can only be through more debt-based money issue. Capitalist market economies are dependent on these circuits of debt-based money (Graziani 2003) and as the financial crisis has shown, the whole system judders to a halt if credit, as debt, is not forthcoming.

Until comparatively recently, money was a mixture of state-issued fiat money (as coin and notes) and bank-issued money as debt. From the second half of the twentieth century the balance shifted dramatically towards debt-based money issue through the banking system such that 'the creation of money is essentially tied to bank credit' (Rossi 2007:21). With the dominance of bank-created 'debt money' the seigniorage benefit of money to the state disappears. States are therefore forced into higher taxation or more borrowing from the private financial system. However seigniorage has not entirely disappeared, it has changed location. Banks can benefit financially as they create new money and lend it. Also, those who can make more money investing or speculating than it costs to borrow money are also exercising seigniorage. The shift to the issue of money through the privately owned banking system has also removed from the public sector any direct control over the direction of money use. This means

exit social morality.

that those who take on debt are making vital choices about the direction of the economy and, as the financial crisis reveals, those choices can rebound on society as a whole.

Bank Credit and Fresh Air Money

The most important aspect of the shift to money issue through bank debt is that banks can lend money they don't have. The basic roles of a bank are usually seen as taking savings deposits and keeping them safe; acting as an intermediary between those who owe money and those who require payment and acting as intermediary between those who have savings and those who need money, that is, those who need to borrow. On these services the bank makes a profit from the difference between what is paid to the depositor and what is received from the borrower. In the process of making loans the bank must be careful to keep sufficient funds to pay out any deposits that are requested: it must hold a reserve. However most of the deposits the bank receives are placed 'on demand'. Theoretically every depositor could turn up asking for their money and the bank would have to pay out regardless of what loans it had outstanding. If money was based on a scarce resource as commodity theorists claimed, the bank would very quickly run out of gold to make loans and depositors would not be able to demand their gold back until the loan was repaid. However, as Galbraith observed, bank money can be in two places at once (1975:19). Paradoxically, it can be lent out and yet it can still be paid back on demand to the depositor. It is the nature of money as an intangible social form that makes this possible. Steve Keen argues that neo-classical theorists continue to theorise banking as barter between savers and borrowers (2001:289) despite the fact that no matter how much the bank lends out, individual savers can still get their money back on demand.

In effect the bank is creating loans out of fresh air. Anyone who takes on debt is creating new money. In Galbraith's well-recorded words, 'the process by which banks create money is so simple that the mind is repelled. Where something so important is involved, a deeper mystery seems only decent' (1975:18–19). James Tobin has described bank money creation as 'fountain pen money' (1963:408). The implications of this capacity to create money through the banking system are largely unrecognised, because 'although today the fact that commercial banks create much more money than the government is now explained in every introductory economics text, *its full significance and effects on the economy have still not been sufficiently considered*' (Daly 1999:142 [author's emphasis]). The most important outcome is that money creation is effectively in private hands through commercial decisions in the banking system, while the state retains responsibility for managing and supporting the system, as has become clear through the financial crisis. It is vitally important to make it clear that while society collectively bears ultimate responsibility for the failures of the commercial money creation system, there is no direct public influence on the overall direction of how finance is invested or used.

The fact that banks are creating new money raises questions of social justice. If new money can be created out of fresh air, like fresh air it should be seen as a resource available to everyone. From a social justice perspective such resources should be shared, or at least their availability should be open to democratic consideration. As Chick points out, 'money confers on those with authority to issue new money the power to pre-empt resources' (1992:141).

Much of this book will be concerned with the implications of this situation. Far from being a social resource, money is currently being mainly created and harnessed by the capitalist system.

Bank Credit and Capitalism

There is a clear connection between the privatisation of money creation and the emergence of capitalism. Money is a social relation that makes possible 'both market exchange and the more extensive set of relationships known as capitalism' (Smithin 2009:59). However, it is banking and the capacity of virtually unlimited creation of money through debt that enabled capitalist expansion. For Ingham 'the essence of capitalism lies in the elastic creation of money by means of readily transferable debt' (2004:108). For full elasticity of credit to be available it is necessary that the creation of bank money breaks free of the limitation of matching loans to deposits. Far from money representing prior market activities as the barter theorists claimed, it is the prior issuing of bank credit that is essential to bringing profit-seeking activities into being. Capitalism would collapse if everyone paid their debts, or if no further debts were taken out. Despite this, there is not extensive radical analysis of the capitalist banking system. As Smithin argues: 'Marxian theory does not deal at all adequately with the role of the banking system and credit creation' (2009:12). This is particularly important since, as Ingham points out, capitalist finance is not without its own contradictions: 'money is socially constructed as a reality in a process of conflict and struggle' (2004:203). This conflict is between those capitalists who hold money and lend it and those productive capitalists who need that finance. The state is also party to that struggle. As Ingham points out, 'the state and the market share in the production of capitalist credit money' (Ingham 2004:144). However, in the last resort it is the state that is the most important. The elastic creation of credit-money is based on a 'hierarchy of debtors' which is topped by the state's total liability for the system in its 'high-powered money'. Without this structure of finance, capitalism cannot operate. In a crisis the state must step in.

Conclusion

Money is an intriguing phenomenon with tremendous power in human societies. Despite some historic use of precious metals, most money in history has not had intrinsic value, nor does it emerge 'naturally' from market activities. Money is socially and politically created by a combination of public, private and social actions. The money system combines an agreed unit of measurement with trust that the money-token or record representing that measurement will be honoured in a future transaction. The notion of the intrinsic value of money through association with precious metals is misleading. What matters is that people agree their financial obligations and then follow them through. From this perspective, money and the market are both social phenomena. While social relationships are sufficient to enable money-based interaction on a personal scale, for money to obtain wider trust it needs to be supported by an institutional authority. If people are to accept a token in return for goods, services or labour, they need to know that someone somewhere will honour that token. This is the role played by the state in recognising money as legal tender and by the banking system in issuing, honouring and circulating money. Money is only as sound as the society and authorities under which it circulates.

Although historically producers and traders privately agreed instruments of credit and debt, the need to have personal relations of trust would have severely limited trade if money was not able to move to a more depersonalised, but still socially recognised, space. This happened through the activities of the state which not only issued most of the coinage in circulation, but also underpinned the money system through its legitimisation of 'high-powered money' represented by the notes and coin in circulation and the deposits of that money within the banking system. The basis of the ability of the state to support the money system rests on its capacity to raise payment for all liabilities through taxation. Despite the importance of the state's role in sustaining the money system, as the issue of money as notes and coins was reduced control of the money system shifted towards the banking sector. Unlike the state which can issue money that does not have to be repaid, banks issue money as debt. All money is a credit or claim upon society, but bank-issued money also carries debt. It has to be paid back with interest. As will be explained more fully in the next chapter, bank-created money as debt is effectively produced out of fresh air. Within a commercial banking system, this means that money creation has been handed to the capitalist system.

Conventional economics has traditionally seen money as reflecting the activities of the market and not as a dynamic force in its own right. Equally, radical thinkers have paid it little attention. However, far from being an adjunct to the market economy, money is an important dynamic in society, possibly the most important one. Money is far too important to be left to the market. If the money system breaks down, societies structured around the issue and circulation of money will not function. This is compounded in contemporary market economies where the emphasis on profit maximisation and cost cutting means that stocks of food and other essentials are kept very low. This leaves very little resilience in the event of a breakdown in the financial system. With low stocks, a collapse in the issue of credit preventing new production could rapidly produce shortages. Therefore, as a provisioning system, the market economy is very vulnerable to a break down in the money circuit.

Following the 2007–08 financial crisis, control of money issue and circulation returned very abruptly to public authorities. States had to attempt to use their authority to stabilise their money systems and in some cases failed. Despite this, state intervention in the financial sector is seen as temporary. States and financial markets alike are aiming for a return to (somewhat more regulated) business as usual. The future is seen as continuing private control of the money creation system, regardless of the fact that it is the commercial dynamics of capitalist finance that created the crisis in the first place. The financial crisis, with its highly active state intervention, provides the opportunity to open up a debate about the nature of money and launch a radical critique of the way that the money system has been privatised under capitalism. The time has come to explore money as a force within human societies. Money may be socially based and publicly supported through the state, but its control currently lies with the profit driven private sector. Understanding and challenging the ownership and control of money within capitalist economies is therefore vital. Far from being a 'private' matter, money should be treated as a public resource and should be used for social purposes, or at least be subject to democratic control. But first it is important to understand how private control of finance emerged in the modern money system. This will be discussed in the next chapter.

T. is doing more than react to CC & PV.
— possibly with out realising it.

2

THE PRIVATISATION OF MONEY

The modern money system has developed as a tangled interaction between the market and the state and central to this has been the role of the banks. Banking, like coinage, is not new: it could go back as far as 3,000 BCE with communal grain stores operating as banks, transferring ownership of deposits between depositors. Central to the modern form of banking is its role in the issue, as well as the circulation, of money. This ability has enabled the commercial sector to gain control of the money system via the banking sector and put the state, and therefore the people, into the role of public debtor. In the process, the commercial creation of debt has slipped from public control although, as the financial crisis shows, not from public liability. While the capitalist financial system has privatised the money system, it remains a system of social trust. The market alone cannot sustain it.

Banking and the State

As Chapter 1 has shown, money in human societies has been created by political authorities or financial entities such as banks or money traders. In the case of banks, paper records of trade became open to wider circulation through the banking system. When traders received a promise to pay or wanted to receive payment immediately on a trade, they could go to a bank with the bill of trade or promissory note and ask the bank to exchange it for one of the bank's own notes. The bank then took on the debt or payment looking to be reimbursed when the trade was completed, or the debt repaid. This service was subject to a fee so that the trader or creditor would be paid less than the face value of the debt, that is, it would be discounted. Banks could also lend money to traders to initiate trade to be repaid with interest. Borrowing money in this way means that the borrower takes on a debt and receives a transferable currency in exchange: 'banking proper can be said to emerge when a bank acquires trade bills by issuing its own banknotes and creating deposits that give the right to withdraw money' (Lapavitsas 2003:79).

The modern banking system brings together private banking in relation to trade and the currency creating powers of the state. At first bankers issued their own transferable currency as credit notes drawn on the bank, but as money issue and banks became more regulated, the money the bank issued was declared legal tender, that is, universally recognised money authorised by the state. Through this process privately generated debts in the market sector were being turned into transferable state money through the banking system. Banks took in commercial paper and issued state authorised money in its place. The significance of this is vital. Commercial debt issued between traders is a liability on the commercial issuer. Commercial debt exchanged for bank-issued money is a liability on the bank. Commercial debt exchanged for bank money that is recognised as legal tender is a liability on the state. As explained in Chapter 1, money is a claim upon society. All monies designated in legal tender are therefore a claim upon society and that claim in the last instance must be honoured by the state. State endorsement of bank debt means that 'banks are... able to issue liabilities at will' (Parguez and Seccareccia 2000:105).

Being able to issue money is a very important political and economic resource. When most money was issued as cash this was mainly regulated by a political authority and gave the issuing authority seigniorage. Whether the money was made from mined metals such as gold or silver, shells, tally sticks or paper, having the monopoly of issue provided interest-free, and virtually cost-free, expenditure. Monarchs and other leaders therefore kept very close control of currency issue. Banks or mints have been licensed and carefully regulated. Monarchs could use the minting system to call in all their currency every few years and either reissue it, taking the opportunity to extract a tax by offering less new coins than the old ones taken in, or reduce the level of precious metal in each coin through debasement (Spufford 1988:289). The power of the issuer is not limitless however, as debased coinage or devalued money can lose public confidence.

Modern states still create money through notes and coin but this is now very limited in comparison with money issue through debt. In Britain it has been calculated that notes and coin only account for around 3 per cent of total money issued while the rest emerges through the banking system as 'sight' accounts, that is, money recorded in bank accounts rather than physical currency (Robertson and Bunzl 2003:19). This shift between publicly-issued fiat money and bank-issued debt-based money has happened comparatively recently. Until the 1960s coin and notes still accounted for around a fifth of money issue (Rowbotham 1998:309). There are two important implications of this change. First, unlike state-issued 'fiat' money which, when issued, becomes the property of the receiver to dispose of as they will, money issued by banks has to be paid back with interest. Second, control of money issue passes from the state to the banking sector and with it the benefits of seigniorage, that is, financial profit from making loans (Robertson and Bunzl 2003:27). For those who borrow, seigniorage is any financial benefit gained from the money over and above the cost of borrowing it. The shifting balance of money issue to the commercial sector was accompanied by an ideological defeat for any conception of public money. Money is seen as something that should be solely connected to the market and commerce. It is not without irony that the market claims the monopoly of wealth creation and describes this as making money. Through the banking sector this is what it quite literally does.

Banks, States and Debt

The early Italian banks lent extensively to monarchs and other rulers, pending income from rents and taxes: 'it was the simple fact of taxation...that provided the basis for the earliest systems of public debt in medieval Italy' (Ferguson 2002:111). This gave the commercial lenders a direct link to taxation and other authorised income which exists to this day. Bank lending to states meant that states, rather than issue their own currency, were borrowing from privately owned money sources. This was the basis on which the Bank of England was created. The Bank of England was set up in 1694 when King William approached the London goldsmiths for a loan of £1.2 million to finance his war against France. As many goldsmiths had been ruined by the Stuart kings not paying previous loans, they refused to lend the money to the king directly. Instead, they demanded an Act of Parliament to establish a Bank of England that would be owned by a private consortium of lenders. This bank would provide the sum of £1.2 million to the state rather than directly to the king. This meant that if the king defaulted the state was liable to repay the loan, that is, it became a debt on the nation. Since that date the national debt has remained a permanent feature of the British economy. As Blain (1987) argues, when a government borrows money it gives away its sovereignty to its creditors. The creation of the national debt put the wealthy in charge of the state's own money supply and therefore in a position of influence over the political direction of the country. The 8 per cent annual interest demanded by the Bank of England financiers meant new taxes of £100,000 a year were needed to pay the interest.

The merchants who formed the Bank of England also turned the promise of a steady income from the loan to the state into the basis for further private credit issue. On the strength of the promised repayment of the £1.2 million they had lent to the king (via the state) they created the same amount of debt to be lent commercially (Galbraith 1975:31). The first initial investment therefore yielded two income streams, one from the state and one from private borrowers. The bank also operated as a normal commercial bank and took deposits and discounted bills of trade. Other commercial banks in England issued notes under their own name, but eventually the Bank of England gained sole control over the issue of notes and coins. In 1946 the Bank was nationalised. Although it was formally made independent of the state in 1997, the Bank of England remains the lender of last resort with responsibility for managing the country's money supply and, as has been made clear, acts via the state as guarantor for the whole banking system.

The founding constitution of the United States enabled it to both borrow and 'to coin money and regulate the value thereof'. Blain (1987) claims that it was the influence and financial interests of the banker Alexander Hamilton, the first US Secretary of the Treasury, that led to a decision by the first US Congress to raise money through a national debt, rather than to issue money directly. The War of Independence had already created a debt of $40 million which, with interest, had risen to $75 million. Many people held war loan debt including members of Congress. It was decided that these would be exchanged for stock in the proposed US bank that would manage this debt. This was established in 1790. Blain alleges that congressmen bought up war loan debts at below face value before the bank proposals were announced, an early example of insider dealing.

The alternative approach to state funding was taken by Abraham Lincoln when he was faced with bankers asking for 30 per cent interest on loans to fight the Civil War. Instead of borrowing at these rates he chose to create $450million directly in the form of 'greenback' dollars which were debt and interest free (Galbraith 1975:93). However, over time the debt-based money creation system prevailed and the interlinking of private banking with money issue became central to the evolution of the Anglo-American capitalist market system. Rather than issue money, governments issued bonds against their debt and major banks such as Barings and Rothschild became major bond dealers (Ferguson 2002:120–21). The Rothschild family, in particular, were major funders of state activities, including wars, across Europe. Nathan Rothschild alone turned capital of £20,000 into a fortune of over £50 million (Rowbotham 1998:199). The increasing reliance by governments on borrowing put states both economically and politically in the hands of capitalist finance. Meanwhile, the ability to create 'credit' as debt enabled the privatised banking system to provide the loans necessary to fund capitalist development.

Money Creation and the Banking System

Banks are strange creatures in that the money they take in as deposits or investments are liabilities and their loans are assets. The presumption is that banks are intermediaries between savers and borrowers, but in practice this is not the case. The basic idea that banks lend the money that savers have deposited, in some relationship of loans to deposits, misunderstands how banking works. One remarkable aspect of banks is that they can lend out money they don't have, that is, they can lend much more money than the deposits they have in total. This is known as fractional reserve banking. If banks held on to all their deposits there could be no loans. If banks lent out all their money they would not be able to return deposits when they were requested. The compromise is a fractional reserve. The bank retains sufficient money to meet reasonable demand. Even then this concept implies some physical limit, as if money were a tangible thing. As money is mostly intangible, and even in the case of notes and coin there is no physical limit, unlike for instance stocks of gold, the concept of a reserve is really an accounting term.

It is the nature of money as a social form that makes this possible. Money can be in two places at once, as Galbraith pointed out, because of its intangibility (1975:19). Money works because it is not gold and limited by its physical properties. This is why, as Keen argues, it is a mistake to see banking as a barter between savers and borrowers (2001:289). Theoretically every bank account holder, including those taking out loans, could turn up asking for their money and the bank would have to pay out, regardless of what loans it had outstanding. If money was based on a precious and limited resource such as gold the banking system would very quickly run out of reserves and depositors would not be able to retrieve their money until some loans were repaid. Paying interest would also be difficult: where would the new gold to pay interest come from if there was a fixed capacity of the money resource?

Nevertheless, banks do have to meet daily demands for both cash withdrawals and to settle surplus transfers to other banks. The fractional reserve can be held in cash or assets near to cash, including a reserve balance lodged with the central bank. Traditionally, lending has been seen as proportional to the fractional reserve and this enables the mechanism of money creation. If the bank is required to keep a 10 per cent reserve, it can lend 90 per cent of any money deposited. However, once a loan is issued, it becomes a new deposit of money that circulates within the banking system, unless someone sends the money abroad or buries it in a pit. As the new money circulates it forms new deposits which become the basis of further loans. These in turn circulate as new deposits fuelling further loans. If the ratio of 1:10 is maintained the original sum will increase nine-fold. It is therefore impossible to disentangle deposits and loans. Since money is lent in relation to total deposits which also includes previous loans, money is effectively created out of fresh air as 'loans can never be financed by some pre-existing deposits' (Parguez and Seccareccia 2000:106–7).

Privately-issued bank money is therefore no more tangible in origin than the publicly-issued fiat money of the state. In fact, the key to the flexibility of bank-issued money is that it is independent of deposits: 'This *creation* of credit-money by lending in the form of issued notes and bills, which exist independently of any particular level of incoming deposits, is the critical development that Schumpeter and others identified as the *differentia specifica* of capitalism' (Ingham 2004:115). 'If banks could not issue money they could not carry on their business' (Innes 1914/2004:53). 'Credit creation is the actual business of banking' (Smithin 2009:66). Schumpeter himself pointed out that until the 1920s economists didn't really understand how banks created money (Daly 1999:142). For modern banking to work effectively it must be based on something that has no natural limits, such as base metal coin, paper notes or sight accounts, that is, those that are a matter of written or electronic record.

As James Tobin has pointed out, 'a long line of financial heretics have been right in speaking of "fountain pen money" – money created by the stroke of the bank president's pen when he approves a loan and credits the proceeds to the borrower's checking account' (1963:408). Victoria Chick defines bank deposits as 'privately issued forms of money' (1992:141) and Daly argues that 'money creation has become a source of private income' (Daly 1999:141). If the contemporary banking system based on elastic credit creation is not determined by prior deposits, then there are no limits to its money creation capacity other than those imposed by accounting conventions and regulatory authorities. However such a potentially unlimited system is still underpinned by centralised authoritative 'high powered' money, that is, the resource of currency or tax revenue available through the state (Smithin 2009:67). While the privatised banking sector has harnessed money creation for itself through the issue of debt, the state still remains as the final basis on which the whole tottering system rests (Wray 2004:260).

Making debt-based money the main source of money issue and circulation creates major problems for economic systems. Debts must be repaid, and at interest. Paying annual interest means that long term debts such as mortgages repay several times the original sum. For green economists this entails destructive pressure for continuing growth and expansion in the economy (Douthwaite 2000:30, Scott Cato 2009:38). Equally, as debt-based money always threatens the provisioning of society it can never be the basis of a sustainable economy (Hutchinson et al. 2002:41). It is also problematic for capitalist economies: profitable circulation of money depends on continual issue of new debt. If the debt cycle ceases it is disastrous for capitalism. In fact, it was the halting of lending between banks that launched the 2007–08 financial crisis. Banks would no longer give credit to each other because they no longer believed in the financial products they were exchanging and therefore they no longer believed in the viability of the banks themselves. Blain argues that creating money as debt means that repayment of debt always threatens the money supply in the absence of any other form of money creation (1987). Keynes had argued that government expenditure was essential if slumps were to be avoided, but the monetarist and neo-liberal arguments of the 1980s and 1990s overwhelmed Keynesian economics and any justification for a government role.

Confidence. Self-belief. health. productivity.
enough. excess.
THE PRIVATISATION OF MONEY **39**
doubt, greed, fear addiction.

Neo-liberal tub thumpers should have looked to history. As Blain records, when governments tried to pay off the national debt it caused a shortage of money. Blain gives the example of Andrew Jackson who vetoed the second renewal of the charter of the Bank of the United States and reduced the federal debt to $38,000 in 1836. This caused a collapse in money supply that created a deep depression in 1837.

The eclipse of a substantial public role in money issue means that the people, individually and through the state, are being made to repay with interest commercially generated fresh air money when they could have created the money out of fresh air for themselves. This is very hard for people schooled in the ideology and practice of capitalist economics to take on board. The ideological claims for private control as against public control of money issue will include accusations such as potential mismanagement, inflationary pressures and inefficiency. These claims of market efficiency ring hollow in the light of the almost unlimited issue of bank credit, following 1980s deregulation. Warburton argues that the Anglo-Saxon economies lost control of credit creation in the 1980s and this was the basis of the impressive performance of global equity markets in the boom years (1999:8). This should not happen according to the 'endogenous' theory of money creation which argues that producers call forth money in order to launch the circuit of production. In what Rossi calls the 'monetary production economy' (2007:32) bank deposits are created by firms 'monetising' their production costs since 'if there were no workers to remunerate bank deposits could not exist...as there would be no production at all and financial markets would be meaningless' (Rossi 2007:34). The new money issued pays the cost of production, this is then repaid in the process of exchange and consumption, and the circle turns again.

On this basis there should never be a problem of money inflation as the new money would always be accompanied by new production and consumption. However, it is clear that in the late twentieth and early twenty-first centuries, the bank credit creation system was not just responding to the needs of production but to the demands of speculative inflation. It is notable that Rossi does not address the possibility of borrowing for pure speculation: 'we leave financial speculation aside, as at the end of any purely speculative...transaction there is always consumption' (Rossi 2007:122). While neo-liberal ideology would quickly pounce on the possibility of the state borrowing or creating money, citing the problem of inflation, the massive issue of credit for speculative finance went largely unremarked. It was no less inflationary, but this was presented as 'wealth creation'. Certainly it made many people very rich and some of the money found its way in to state coffers through tax. However, as states were receiving the product of uncontrolled credit creation, the public would eventually have to pay the price in its role as guarantor of the money system.

From Regulation to Deregulation

Shifting money creation from the public sector to the private sector does not make it any less a social phenomenon or public responsibility. As has become evident in the financial crisis, the benefits of privatised money creation have accrued to capitalist speculators (as will be discussed in Chapter 4), while the state and the population have to pay the price. During its history the banking system has seen many failures. Many of these have followed periods of speculation (Kindleberger 1996:20). This was particularly so after the Great Depression when thousands of banks failed. Among the causes of failure was the use of bank loans to speculate on the stock market and banks speculating themselves, known as proprietary trading. One of the key reforms in the US was to separate deposit-taking retail banks from other financial services, including investment. This was enacted under the Glass Steagall Act of 1933. Britain did not have a similar ruling, but prior to the 1980s financial institutions were regulated as to what they could charge and the conditions under which they could lend. This was particularly the case with mortgages (Glyn 2007:54). They were also required to maintain substantial reserves. The wider money system was equally carefully controlled with national currencies subject to fixed exchange rates and exchange controls.

The regulatory system began to break down in the early 1970s for several reasons. One was the collapse of the Bretton Woods system of fixed exchange rates as national currencies started to break free of their national boundaries. This was particularly true of the dollar, where due to the purchase of oil in dollars, large amounts of dollars were held outside the USA. Eventually these 'euro-dollars' started to be circulated through the global banking system. Governments found they could not control their boundaries against the movement of currencies and had to abandon control on the movement of money. Credit restrictions were also lifted. In 1971, the Conservative government in Britain released credit controls in a 'dash for growth'. This led to a mushrooming of 'fringe' banks and a commercial property and house price boom. In November 1973 one of the new banks, London and County Securities, collapsed and the whole fringe 'secondary' banking system started to unravel. Even some of the mainstream banks were threatened. The collapse was triggered when the government raised interest rates to curb inflation following the quadrupling of oil prices after the 1973 Yom Kippur war. The outcome was two years of recession with high levels of inflation and several banks having to be supported by the Bank of England. It might be thought that lessons would have been learned, but similar crises and bailouts occurred throughout the next 30 years, interspersed with periods of debt driven prosperity.

Disregarding this history, the push for less bank regulation continued particularly in Britain and the USA. Reagan substantially deregulated the financial sector while Margaret Thatcher launched her 'Big Bang' in 1986. This unleashed a wave of speculative investments in real estate and risky high interest 'junk bonds'. Bank failures were not far behind. The US's Citibank had to be rescued with $1.5 billion of Saudi cash in 1989. Johnson Matthey bank in Britain and Continental Illinois in the US had to be nationalised. In the late 1980s the US Savings and Loans organisations fell victim to speculative losses and had to be bailed out. In 1991 Britain saw the collapse of another fringe bank, BCCI, the implications of which were still being unravelled in 2008. Despite these problems, the Glass Steagall legislation was being challenged. In 1997 Citibank merged with the insurance group Travelers which breached the US ruling that banks should not cross-sell financial products (Scurlock 2007). Following intense lobbying, the Clinton administration finally rescinded the Glass Steagall Act in 1999. The Financial Services Modernisation Act freed banks to embrace a wide range of financial activities: banking, insurance, mortgages, stock market trading, personal and speculative lending and bank direct investment.

Europe had always allowed 'universal' banks, but there had been restrictions which banks agitated to be removed. The central problem for the traditional banking sector was pressure from competition for their savings and loans market. From the 1970s the high street banks' basic business became less viable as people started to invest and borrow from a wider range of financial institutions. In this process of 'disintermediation' (Langley 2002:22) banks ceased to be the primary vehicle for people's money as they turned to other forms of saving, such as pensions or investment funds (Langley 2006:919). Large companies were also raising their own loans and even developing financial services themselves, such as consumer credit. In the 1950s nearly 50 per cent of new US savings went into banks, with around a third going into investment funds. By 1994 virtually none was going into banks and more than 70 per cent into investment funds (Warburton 1999:95). Consumer credit, credit cards, mortgages, insurances and stock market investments were expanding rapidly. By 2008 US regulated banks only accounted for a quarter of total credit (Wray 2008:7). In Britain, high street banks could no longer rely on the steady inflow of customers' savings and borrowings and began to agitate for more flexibility. They were allowed to broaden the scope of their lending, most notably to mortgages which put the traditional building societies under pressure. This drove a process of demutualisation where building societies converted from being mutuals to become commercial banks. Abbey National led the move early on in 1988, others held on but the late 1990s saw a large number transferring: Alliance and Leicester, Woolwich, Bradford and Bingley, Halifax,

Northern Rock, Bristol and West, National and Provincial all transferred in 1997.

Liquidity and Solvency

As banks lend disproportionately to their deposits, and are always facing a potential demand for cash or excess bank transfers, they are in continual danger of problems of liquidity and solvency. Liquidity means having enough ready money to meet immediate demands for withdrawals. Solvency means the overall assets of the bank (which are mainly held in the form of loans and investments) are sufficient to meet its overall liabilities (which are mainly to savers, investors or creditors). While there are no physical, or even accountancy, limits to money creation provided the books balance, the system is always unstable. The financial system, as a capitalist system, is one that must always be in forward motion. If it falters it will collapse. The dilemma for banks is that they 'borrow short and lend long'. This is because the deposits they take are returnable on demand while loans will not return until they are due. Banks, therefore, have a fatal combination of small reserves, illiquid assets and returnable bank deposits, with everything depending on depositor confidence (Warburton 1999:54). As Martin Wolf of the *Financial Times* put it, if we were not so familiar with banking we would surely treat the notion of borrowing 'short and safe' in order to lend 'long and risky' as fraudulent' (20 March 2009).

The way banks deal with the problem of liquidity is by holding a certain proportion of ready assets in cash or near cash. This is often held through an account at the central bank. That leaves the question of the level of reserves needed. For much of the twentieth century the regulatory norm was 10–12 per cent. From the 1980s under the Basle rules it was around 8 per cent, however as lending expanded the ratio dropped much lower. Speaking in 2008, D'Arista calculated that prevailing US bank reserves covered less than one-tenth of one per cent of deposits, compared with 11 per cent in 1951 (D'Arista 2008). Calculating what should form the basis of a reserve, and what it should be held against, is complex and has been the subject of negotiations through the international banker's organisation, the Bank for International Settlements (BIS) in Basle. BIS has struggled to find a means of defining how a bank's reserve should be calculated. A BIS Accord in the late 1980s proposed an 8 per cent 'Tier 1' reserve as a combination of capital assets and cash deposits. However, as banks began to operate in new ways in the deregulated environment the composition of the bank balance sheets became much more complex. A 'Tier 2' level of reserves was identified that sought to match different types and level of reserve to the varied liabilities and viability of assets. In response Basle II allowed banks some extent of self-regulation, including the use of agency ratings and devising their own risk assessment models (Wade 2008:20).

The idea of a reserve is seen as meaningless by Steve Keen, particularly where this is represented by reserve deposits lodged at the central bank. He argues that such a reserve does not exist, but is simply represented by another layer of credit issued by the central bank. Keen argues that, in practice, far from the text-book model of the level set by the central bank reserve system driving the level of loans, the central reserve bank has to follow the clearing banks' lead by creating a suitable notional reserve to back money issue:

> Rather than the State directly controlling the money supply via its control over the issue of new currency and the extent to which it lets banks leverage their holdings of currency, private banks and other credit-generating institutions largely force the State's hand. (Keen 2001:303)

Lapavitsas and Saad-Filho argue that the central bank must always respond to the quantity of loans made in the banking system as these are driven by requests from borrowers who are engaged in the productive system. When firms request loans to start the productive cycle and banks create these *ex nihilo*, that is, out of fresh air, this determines the money supply. Given that the loans have already been made, the central bank, if requested, cannot refuse to back these loans if the system is to maintain its viability, 'consequently, the central bank cannot control the quantity of base money...loans make deposits, deposits make reserves, and credit money determines base money' (Lapavitsas and Saad-Filho 2000:311–12). As Lapavitsas argues, the central bank as the apex of the pyramid of the credit system is effectively banker to the money market (2003:84). Despite the fact that bank credit 'has the most clearly social character in a capitalist economy' Lapavitsas is quite clear whose interests would prevail in a crisis. As the central bank is a creature of the capitalist credit system 'at times of crisis…the broader interests of society are subordinated to the needs and demands of the credit system' (Lapavitsas 2003:86).

With limited direct means of issuing money, the state through the central bank has two main instruments: open market operations and interest rates. Open market operations involves the buying and selling of government bonds to control the overall money supply. Selling bonds decreases money supply, buying back bonds increases money supply. Interest rates aim to encourage or discourage the issue of new money by making money more or less expensive. Banks are expected to follow base rate guidance. However in the financial crisis even this mechanism failed in the UK, when the interbank rate of lending (LIBOR) broke free of the central bank and did not follow a base rate reduction. LIBOR is the basis on which banks interact with each other in the money markets. The British Bankers' Association London Interbank Offer Rate is calculated daily for ten currencies and for 15 different time periods from overnight to 12 months. MacKenzie argues that LIBOR 'matters more than any other set of numbers in the world' and controls contracts of around $300 trillion (2008:237).

The problem with trying to control bank lending through interest rates is that they are slow and reactive. As any shift in interest rates takes some time to work through and central banks, in any event, are often fighting the last battle, they find themselves 'behind the curve'. In reacting to inflation, central banks increase interest rates which can cause recessions. In times of recession they lower interest rates which can increase credit and threaten speculative booms. Speaking on the BBC Today programme (28 September 2007) Alan Greenspan, who headed the US Federal Reserve from 1987 to 2006, acknowledged that central banks find it very difficult to resolve financial problems because these cannot be anticipated. He also admitted that central banks don't really have control over interest rates and cannot control large flows of capital worldwide. Greenspan was a cheerleader for the free market and was praised for helping the US out of the dotcom collapse and the post 9/11 crisis by lowering interest rates. However, many of the problems that the world economy now faces developed under his regime. Reflecting later, Greenspan talked of his 'big mistake', which was not realising that banks might not act in the long term interests of their shareholders or even their businesses (Tett 2009:297). This would not have surprised John Kenneth Galbraith who remarked on the low quality of people who manage money and the fact that 'failure is almost never at a cost to those responsible' (1975:302).

A central task of bank regulation is to ensure that the financial system is solvent and not fraudulent. When Labour came to power in 1997 the regulatory system was reformed and the Bank of England was given independent control of monetary policy. A tripartite system was set up with regulation split between the Treasury, the Bank of England and the newly-created Financial Services Authority. The Financial Services Authority monitored individual banks while the Bank of England had responsibility for managing the money supply. Unfortunately neither of the organisations nor the Treasury had oversight of the overall integrity of the financial system. For most of the 1990s and early 2000s the banking system seemed to be able to do no wrong. Banking shares led the stock markets, financial assets were rising and more and more people were able to access credit. There were insurances for depositors in place and the market seemed to be self-regulating. However, innovations within the financial system were developing that no-one, least of all the supervisory system, were able to understand or control.

Innovations in Banking: Securitised Finance

One of the major changes in the banking system came with a shift from money lending and circulation through the banking system to money circulation through the money market. The money market brings together all those wanting to borrow money and all those with money to lend. The growth of the money market was a response to the huge amounts of money that had been created and were now circulating looking for a home. This included savings from resource rich or trading surplus countries such as the oil states and China, and companies, institutions and investors generally looking for higher returns. Money was seeking a way to make more money, but with so much ready money available, there was a limit to where viable investments could be found. This led to what looked like a virtuous circle. Relieved of credit restrictions, banks were running up against the formal limits of their balance sheets. They were also finding it difficult to generate sufficient profit even with the volume of credit they were creating.

The neat solution appeared to be to sell the debt on to the money market. Banks began to tap into the flow of money available by selling the debts they were issuing as an asset for investment, that is, as a security. Like the traders who once swapped the debts they held for ready bank money, banks started to swap the debts they held for ready money market finance. Investors would buy bank debt at a discount and receive a profit as the loans matured. This was a tremendous benefit for the banks' balance sheet because whereas in the past banks kept the loans they made on their books, now they were sold on and were therefore 'off balance sheet' and did not count against any lending ratios or against profits. More importantly, instead of loans that were slowly being paid off, the banks had more ready cash to expand their business. The more debts the banks sold on the more profit they made against capital. In the end it was not the need for loans that drove the market, but the need to find loans to soak up all the investment available for securities and thereby make more profit.

The process of 'securitisation', whereby debts were packaged up and sold on as asset-based securities, was very much a US innovation because the US, and particularly its investment banks, were responsible for 80 per cent of all securitisations (Phillips 2008:97). It was a market that grew very rapidly from the 1980s onwards. In 1990 Citicorp converted future credit card interest

into marketable bonds and between 1985 and 1995 the US securitisation market grew from $600bn to $2000 billion (Ingham
2004:221n7). The process was known as 'originate to distribute'.
Lenders originated the debt and then distributed it via the securitisation process to the market. Debt buying became 'the new
frontier, the Wild West of the financial world...the fastest growing
business on Wall Street' (Scurlock 2007:27). Selling of debt was
applied to all sorts of lending activities but the most notable, and
the one that contributed to the downfall of the banking system,
was mortgages. Through securitisation, the income stream from
mortgage loans could be traded as a financial investment. Between
1990 and 2006 the amount of residential debt processed by issuers
of asset-based securities increased from $55 billion to $2,117
billion (Panitch and Konings 2009:75). The securities went under
a variety of names: mortgage backed securities (MBS), asset-based
securities (ABS) and collateralised debt obligations (CDOs).

Mortgage backed securities seemed to be a good, safe asset
because the history of mortgage lending had shown it to be
relatively free of risk. Mortgage lending since World War II,
particularly in the US, had been very stable with no history
of major defaults. The house price boom also seemed to be
unending and any debts that might occur would be covered by
the rising value of the property. This innovative way of raising
money seemed to offer almost unlimited funding and profitable
investment. Securitisation developed dramatically in the housing
market during the 1990s, but particularly after 2000. At the time
of the credit crunch in August 2007 funds for between a half and
two-thirds of British mortgages were being raised in the money
markets as 'wholesale funds', whereas before 1990 more than
two-thirds of mortgages were linked to savings deposits, mainly
through building societies.

In order to avoid the remnants of the regulatory regime and
liquidity limits, banks organised the new activities in what was
effectively a 'shadow' banking system. Semi-detached 'structured
investment vehicles' (SIV) were set up to administer the securities
issued. Investment banks played a very large part in setting up the
securitised loans and this brought them into a very close working

relationship with retail banks and other mortgage lenders. Phillips sees the structures of the shadow banking system as 'liquidity factories' creating 'candyfloss money' (2008:185). As a result of the seemingly unlimited amount of money available through this process, the lending criteria became more and more lax. A lot of money was to be made at all levels from the initiator of the 'originate to distribute' process, through those who packaged up the loans, to those who invested in them. This led to a build up of subprime loans which were initially attractive to investors because they paid higher rates of interest. Any residual risk would be overcome by another innovation of the new system. As well as tapping into the wider money market, the securitisation of mortgage debt would mean that any risk was spread among many investors through CDOs, that is, collatoralised debt obligations.

Collatoralised debt obligations were packages of mortgages that included both prime and subprime loans. These were presented in the form of 'structured finance' that was 'sliced and diced'. This meant that bundles of mortgages could be sold to different investors at different rates of interest. Institutional investors such as insurance companies and pension funds were offered less profit margin, but were the first to be paid out in the event of any loss overall. A second level could be offered which would be paid out second and so on, down to the most risky that would be paid out last and was priced to give a very high rate of profit. Each investor therefore knew the risk they seemed to be taking. However, even the most risky level of investment was still receiving high credit ratings from the rating agencies because, even though they contained subprime debt, mortgages were seen as an unproblematic area of investment. Also the organisations selling the finance had good ratings and the icing on the cake was that the debt was insured. Alongside the structured finance was a framework of guarantees against non-payment from well-established insurers. In recognition of these facts MBSs were given the top rating of security (Triple A) by the rating agencies. Scurlock has described this process as 'mortgage laundering' (2007:87).

What no-one took account of at the time was that mortgages were being sold in dubious ways. People were being pressured into taking out mortgages, ability to pay was not verified and people were offered deals that seemed very good, but only lasted a short time. In the US in particular, people had been used to long term fixed rate mortgages and were very confused by a shift to mortgages with adjustable rates. Also, mortgage companies knew they could sell on the product very quickly and, therefore, any risk would be off their balance sheets. Under the 'originate to distribute' model of lending it was difficult, if not impossible, to assess or locate risk. Lenders were selling on their loans in complicated packages that made any risk that went with them unclear. The problem of risk was addressed by yet another financial innovation, Credit Default Swaps (CDS). For a fee, insurers would provide cover against the risk of default.

As there was no organised market for such arrangements, these tended to be private 'over-the-counter' arrangements between organisations. Because they were private unregulated arrangements the only security the 'counter-parties' had was that the insurers and sellers were both rated Triple A. This had the effect of making the debts themselves seem safe. The credit insurance market rapidly became one of the biggest growth areas of the new regime. By 2007 total credit lent out and insured in credit default swaps and various other credit derivatives reached over $60 trillion, according to the International Swaps and Derivatives Association. Many of these were multiple insurances relating to the same debt, as insurances were sought each time the debt was traded. Finally, problems of debt default in the US subprime mortgage market led to a collapse of the whole shaky edifice of debt-based securities and wholesale finance. This destroyed the optimism and trust which underpinned the whole system resulting in a credit crunch (Brummer 2008, Morris 2008, Turner 2008). Institutions saddled with unknown levels of risk refused to offer any more credit in any direction.

In August 2006 a special issue on banking of the *New Inter-nationalist* magazine (No.392) charged the banking system with mainly investing in the new financial instruments rather than in productive companies or, even less, in small businesses or the billion low-income, self-employed in the world. Banks were not supplying essential financial services such as sending migrant workers' remittances back to their home countries cheaply. Moving such remittances safely and cheaply is essential as they are worth double the size of world aid and are a major contributor to the income of small, poor countries. Instead, banks were helping rich people to avoid tax, the amount of which *New Internationalist* estimates to be equivalent worldwide to the GNP of Hong Kong each year. For some time banks had also been withdrawing from traditional frontline banking services (Leyshon and Thrift 1997:225). Running small accounts and providing local branches was expensive and the push was to rationalise. This meant that poorer communities were left without ready access to bank branches, or even building societies (Fuller and Mellor 2008:1506). In Britain the government tried to encourage banks to set up basic bank accounts for the lower paid, but this was not embraced enthusiastically. Ironically Britain once had a government-owned bank run through post offices, the Giro bank, but under the enthusiasm for privatisation this was sold into the private sector and ceased to exist. Such a bank might not have helped as post offices were also being closed; in fact a major programme of post office branch closures in Britain was only prevented by the financial crisis itself. The crisis has also revived the idea of a PostBank run through post offices.

The new mechanism of raising money and selling debt had profound implications for the banking system. It meant that banks were becoming reliant on securing a constant flow of money from the money markets and were themselves becoming debtors and insurers of debt. The world of finance was also expanding rapidly with a credit fuelled orgy of speculation. John McFall, Chair of the UK Treasury Select Committee, writing in the *Guardian* (9 January 2009) calculated that the 'alternative banking world' of investment banks, hedge funds and money market funds had amassed $10–$12 trillion by early 2007 and produced $500 trillion of complex derivatives. Even if the regulatory authorities had had their eye on the ball, the ball itself had run away from them into the long grass. Presciently in 1999 Warburton warned of the danger that by acting off-balance sheet banks would over-extend themselves and went on to ponder how safe bank deposits would be, let alone bank shares, in this 'brave new world' (1999:69).

Panitch and Konings (2009) challenge the case that poor banking regulation was the cause of the financial crisis. They point out that it was not the fact that governments had failed to regulate, there was still a system of regulation, but that states were complicit in the innovations that took place. For the US they see the global shift to deregulation as not about freeing financial institutions, but consolidating the imperial power of American finance (2009:68). They point out that in 1993 the Clinton administration actually exempted some of the new derivative instruments from regulation (2009:68). Greenspan had been relaxed about the innovative approaches and even after the crash did not advocate the regulation of derivatives (Greenspan 2008:528). As Warburton warned, an extraordinary reversal of roles was taking place where the large developed economies were becoming the servant of a global financial system and not its master. He blamed the central banks for not challenging the financial innovations and for having little regard for global stability in not restraining the growth of global finance (1999:xi–xiii). Panitch and Konings on the other hand, see financialisation as enlarging the international power of the American state through the extension of 'strategic leeway available to capital' but at the same time the state was involved in a 'step-by-step construction of a too-big-to-fail regime' (2009:72). The state and central banks had supported and encouraged the new banking system, and its link to the expanded market in money, because they did not understand, or had forgotten, the social and public nature of banking. The financial system is never a private matter, its problems will always rebound on the public.

Private Good; Public Bad

By the late twentieth century, bank created debt had almost totally eclipsed the state in money issue: 'for most practical purposes, the rapid growth of banks' balance sheets is synonymous with the rapid growth of money supply' (Warburton 1999:64). While credit creation in the private sector became almost unlimited, neo-liberal ideology declared that public sector borrowing or a state role in the money system would have a negative impact on 'market forces'. The notion of money creation by the state was associated with hyperinflation and utterly rejected as 'printing money'. Recurrent examples like the hyperinflation in Zimbabwe did not help this perception. An alternative view of the cause of inflation is that it is not the public issue of money in itself that is the problem, but issuing it in an unbalanced way so that consumer demand is not matched by material wealth in the production of goods and services. Parguez and Seccareccia see this as the cause of the pre-war German hyperinflation (2000:107). In the case of Zimbabwe this was clearly a failed state whose productive system had collapsed. Its hyperinflation and debased money was arguably as much a reflection as a cause of its predicament. The fact that through history public authorities have created and circulated money without necessarily incurring inflationary consequences is ignored as, too, is the historical evidence of disastrous activities by banks. In the privatised world of private good, public bad, the public sector has been forced to meet expenditure by borrowing from commercially created and circulated money.

The banking and financial sector, on the other hand, has been able to borrow and circulate money almost without limit. Failing to see that commercial money creation was behind the flood of money in the new financial world, bankers and financiers congratulated themselves on the amount of money they were making. This gave rise to a culture of paying huge bonuses to city traders and bankers mainly related to the constant inflation of financial asset values, high volumes of trade and, particularly, share price. This fuelled a short term bonus and profit driven business culture regardless of long term risk. As money markets have grown, bringing together a wide range of financial organisations including the banks, the privatised financial system is effectively creating money for itself. The state has a residual regulatory role through the central bank, but is itself just another borrower. While financial institutions continue to buy state debt and trust its ability to pay, the state can create money as a borrower, but the power in the relationship has passed to the creditors, basically the large financial engines of the private sector. States are given credit ratings like other borrowers and can find credit prohibitively expensive or impossible to get. The modern system of money issue has left the direction of the economy almost entirely in private, commercial hands. In Britain this leads to contortions of public policy where investment in the public sector, such as hospitals, were funded by commercial finance through PFI (Private Finance Initiative) schemes leading to increased overall costs in the long term (Pollock 2004:27).

The dominance of the private sector was shown in the construction of the European monetary regime. Central to this was the independence of the European Central Bank from European states with no mechanism for co-ordinated public input. In its founding legislation, the EU central bank cannot lend directly to governments, it can only lend to the financial sector. The euro can only be brought into being by the demands of private agents, states cannot request it. Governments are also limited in their capacity to borrow. Under the EU Stability and Growth pact budget deficits can be no more than 3 per cent of GDP and total borrowing (national debt) must be no more than 60 per cent. As Ingham argues, 'the Maastricht conditions and the single currency represent a triumph of economic orthodoxy – especially the monetary preoccupation with inflation and "sound money"' (2004:192). Gordon Brown in the UK also capitulated to economic orthodoxy by making the Bank of England independent from the state. The US government is also legally unable to create money (Greenspan 2008:515). However, as the financial crisis escalated, these artificial boundaries started to crumble with the need to return monetary responsibility to the public, as represented by the state.

The rejection of any public role in money issue is based on the ideology of the efficiency of the market. All economic wealth is seen as coming from the market and all government borrowing therefore is a drain on private, wealth-creating activities. This assumes that the public sector cannot generate value, that there is no wealth to be had in public and communal activities. If market-based theories of money are right, money represents the vitality of the economy and will rise and fall with market activities. Any mechanism that interferes with the market could throw the money system out of balance. On the other hand, if social, and particularly state, theories of money are correct, if the state cannot engage independently in the money creation and circulation process, the money system has no backstop. Money would have to revert to being a trust between producers, traders, workers and consumers, mediated by bankers. Money would once more be a private instrument, no longer guaranteed by state 'high powered' money, that is, notes, coins and bank deposits designated in publicly authorised currency. Money would still be social in that it would be based on trust, but it would not have public authority.

It may be argued that while banks may have only limited cash reserves, they have assets and capital value to support their balance sheets. However both disappear in a crisis, share prices collapse and assets lose value or, in the case of loans, become unrecoverable. Long before the current crisis Galbraith noted that banks have 'age-old spasms of optimism and feckless expansion' (1975:306) but noted that the public and private could never be separated because 'the problem of money has now become fully coordinate with that of the economy...even the polity' (1975:303). As long as the state still endorses the money system 'money is always fiat money...even...when the role of the state is marginal' (Parguez and Seccareccia 2000:106). Public may be bad in the eye of the market, but it is essential to the money system.

Conclusion

The main focus of this chapter has been the way that money issue and circulation has moved dramatically towards the private sector. This has implications for the control of the money system and for the integrity of the system itself. Capitalism requires a banking system with money creation capacity. The current era of neo-liberal lax banking regulation has presented it with an almost unlimited supply of credit. Banks, as profit driven companies, must seek to maximise profits and when boring safe banking proved not to be profitable, banks sought out more adventurous ways to make money. The result was the securitisation of debt, linked to the growth of money markets which shifted the money system beyond any form of public control. This was fuelled by a growth in financialisation, that is, extensive investment in financial products and the prioritisation of increasing the money value of assets. This was not confined to speculative capitalists, but spread throughout whole economies as will be discussed in the next chapter. Now that the system has gone bad, and the financial products and their underlying debt have turned toxic, many people's economic security is threatened, through pension funds, house prices, jobs and even the circulation of basic goods and services.

As regulatory 'fire-walls' broke down, unregulated banks and non-bank financial institutions became entangled with the regulated banking system. These were supposed to be beyond the state's sphere of responsibility, but as the financial system expanded and the money market grew, all aspects of the financial system became so interlinked that to break it at any point could threaten the whole circuit. Given the entangled nature of the privatised money system, the public as represented by the state cannot avoid becoming involved. Once there is a direct link between the capitalist market and the state via the money system there is effectively no such thing as a private sector. While money creation and circulation is in private hands and used for private benefit, the state still retains responsibility for managing and supporting the system with ultimate responsibility for its functioning. Therefore, society through the public sector collectively bears the consequences of a failure of the capitalist money system, but has no influence on the overall direction of how finance is invested or used.

The most important aspect of control of money through capitalist banks is that there is no public control over the economic priorities it represents. Who pays the piper (on borrowed money) calls the tune in the economy. While public debt is seen as a 'drain' on 'the economy', private debt is welcomed even if the investment is in armaments, rain forest clearance or speculating against the state's own currency. This is even more important given the way that money is created, effectively out of nowhere, as fresh air money. If it were actually fresh air, money would be seen as a public resource to be used for public benefit. It would also be seen as something to be monitored to maintain its quality. As something that has come from nowhere, money should be treated as a public resource and not harnessed for private benefit. One way to challenge the exclusionary, exploitative and destructive effects of capitalism would be to demand that money issue and use be made subject to democratic control, or even (re)claimed wholesale by the public sector. As will be discussed in the final chapter, democratic public control of money issue could be a means of achieving socio-economic change towards a more ecologically sustainable economy.

3

'PEOPLE'S CAPITALISM': FINANCIALISATION AND DEBT

The Anglo-American model of capitalism has been built on globalisation, neo-liberalism and financialisation. This has appeared to bring a superficial prosperity to a substantial minority of the population of dominant economies at the expense of widening inequalities both within individual societies and across the globe. For the more prosperous western economies, globalisation has encouraged rampant consumerism based on the import of cheap goods. Neo-liberalism has encouraged privatised individualism and discouraged public and collective forms of action. Financialisation has increased the dominance of money and money value: 'financialisation means the increasing role of financial motives, financial markets, financial actors and financial institutions in the operation of the domestic and international economies' (Epstein 2005:3). By the late twentieth century the principles of privatisation and financialisation had intruded into the personal lives of the population (Langley 2008). People have been encouraged to 'stand on their own two feet' and see their security in money terms backed by personal financial assets. As concepts such as 'people's capitalism' and 'a property owning democracy' were promoted with ideological fervour, people were encouraged to think that there was 'no such thing as society' and that the state was an interfering nanny stealing their hard-earned money out of their pockets. This undermined public and collective approaches to social solidarity. Collective forms such as trades unions went into decline and hard won social policies such as pensions and various social insurances were undermined.

At the heart of financialisation was the assumption that money can be made out of money and that money in itself can secure a person's economic life. Savings were no longer security for a rainy day, they were investments. A house was no longer a home, but a financial asset. Private investments and the privatisation of public and mutual sector organisations saw a huge influx of people on to the stock market, which appeared to give large parts of the population a stake in the capitalist financial system. As Panitch and Konings argue, financialization 'played a vital domestic role... integrating subordinate classes into a web of financial relations through private pensions, consumer credit and mortgages'. Speaking of the American experience, they point out that far from Polanyi's notion that markets have become disembedded from society, 'neoliberalism and financial expansion...embedded financial forms and principles more deeply in the fabric of American society' (2009:68).

The 'Democratisation' of Debt

Debt has always existed in human societies. As the first two chapters have shown, the issue of money as debt has played an important part in the emergence of the modern money system and, as will be discussed more fully in the next chapter, the development of the capitalist system. However, debt has also proved to be a major source of social and personal problems and has been proscribed by many religions (Pettifor 2006:132). Debt-bondage still occurs in many societies and indebtedness is a problem for many people from poor farmers to economic migrants, the unemployed, low-paid workers and overburdened consumers. The difference between traditional and contemporary debt is that debt has become an established and socially accepted way of life. This has seen generations of young people emerging from universities already heavily in debt. In the expanding economies of the post-war era, to have accrued high levels of debt was not a matter for social concern and shame, but a sign of social status and creditworthiness. This was particularly true as debt became 'credit' and consumer goods were bought on 'hire purchase'. Status symbols such as cars were purchased with loans and there was a massive expansion of mortgage debt through the promotion of home ownership. As the use of credit escalated, retail companies began to make more money through loans than on products. This was particularly true for cars and white goods, with companies like General Electric and General Motors forming highly profitable finance arms.

Credit cards were an important aspect of the new credit boom and the United States and Britain were major users, much more so than mainland Europe. British people hold 70 million credit cards as against, for example, Germany's 2.3 million (Lawson 2009:87). Credit cards were originally developed by companies to encourage corporate loyalty. Oil companies issued the first Diner's Club Card in 1949 and holding one was a status symbol. The VISA card was issued by Bank of America in 1958. At first it was difficult to obtain a credit card, but by the late twentieth century they were a major force for the 'democratisation' of debt, as most people in the US and the UK had at least one. In fact, not to have a credit card became problematic, as it meant that the person concerned did not have a 'credit profile' and therefore might find it difficult to obtain debt finance. Credit card borrowing also meant that large amounts of money were being issued into the economy by consumers as they spent and borrowed. Arguably, this is a form of economic democracy as the consumer's choice will prevail, but this ignores the role of advertising, impulse buying and the problems of those burdened with consumer debts (Lawson 2009:74). As, in Lawson's terms, Britain became an 'all-consuming' society it also became the credit capital of Europe, owing £1.3 trillion by 2008 (Lawson 2009:87). The same pattern emerged in the US where household debt leapt from 70 per cent of disposable income in 1985 to 122 per cent by 2006 (Pettifor 2006:1). This is because debt has been rising much faster than household income. As Scurlock points out, the most recent generation of people has seen US household income rise by only 1 per cent whereas debt has risen by 1,000 per cent (2007:5). As a proportion of GDP, US household debt rose from 50 per cent in 1980 to 100 per cent in 2007 (Gowan 2009:26). There has been much handwringing over the level of debt in society, but as Scurlock points out, the banking system makes much more money by putting people into debt than by encouraging them to save: 'banking is about selling a single product: debt' (2007:46). Ann Pettifor warned in 2006 of the dangers of 'debtonation' where the first world would be mired in debt in the same way that the Third World economies were in the 1980s. She predicted this would result in a deflationary crisis (Pettifor 2006:45).

Selling debt became a major source of profit for the financial services industry. As Ann Pettifor points out, for the early part of the twentieth century, and particularly the post-war period, interest rates were low. However, the new era of deregulated privatised credit has become usurious, particularly for borrowing on credit or store cards with interest charges of up to 30 per cent (Pettifor 2006:76–7). While the early credit cards went to the better off, often with an annual charge, later there was a much less discriminate mass issue of cards. The market became highly competitive with many finance companies becoming involved. Charges were dropped and people were often bombarded with offers of credit. The main source of profit for the credit issuers was the interest and charges on those who did not pay off their card each month. While many credit card holders use their card as a convenient means of payment, many others remain in permanent debt, particularly the less well off. A pattern emerged that was to recur in the housing market: the most profitable borrowers for the credit companies were those least able to pay. Companies started to target the marginal poor who were the most profitable group as they paid higher levels of interest on their debt over longer periods. The inevitable logic was that credit card companies would search out those who were most likely to be 'maxed out' and pay the highest interest rates and penalties on borrowings. There was also an incentive to have as many holders as possible on minimum payments. In the US this is around 12 per cent of holders, while up to 70 per cent of Americans do not pay their credit card bill in full at the end of the month (Scurlock 2007:68). The ideal borrower is the regular defaulter who pays maximum interest and penalty fees, with the latter earning companies up to

$20 billion (Scurlock 2007:22). According to the *Financial Times* (5 August 2009) total US credit card debt was $850 billion and 10 per cent of balances in the US and UK were defaulting.

As a result of the rising levels of credit many people found themselves with levels of debt that were completely unsustainable. One caller to the UK Credit Card Counselling Service owed £225,000 (Lawson 2009:87). Scurlock reports that the US personal bankruptcy rate in the 2007–08 crisis is ten times the level in the Great Depression (2007:5). The evidence is that most of these bankruptcies don't represent profligate expenditure but people, particularly women, trying to keep their head above water. A major cause of indebtedness in the US is borrowing to pay for health care (2007:154). In the UK the Citizens Advice Bureau reported that even before the crisis it was dealing annually with 1.7 million debt problems, averaging more than 6,600 a day (Lawson 2009:160). By 2009 these had risen to more than 9,000 per day.

Lack of appreciation of the difference between secured and unsecured debt has led to many people taking out 'consolidation' loans. These tend to be advertised heavily on daytime TV, where they are more likely to be seen by women. Home owners with unsecured loans have 'consolidated' their loans against their homes, thereby putting their home at risk. Consolidated loans can also lead to people paying up to ten times more than the original sum borrowed as they are paid over a longer period. As levels of debt and default escalated, debt collection became big business. 'Vulture' companies bought debt from banks and other agencies for a small percentage of the face value and then pursued the debtors who could be individuals, households, companies or even states.

While those mired in debt are a major feature of the contemporary economies, there are those for whom credit is even more problematic. For those on very low incomes, borrowing has long been a way of life. Lack of access to affordable credit means that borrowing for the poor is an expensive way of meeting immediate needs (Collard and Kempson 2005). Around a fifth of all households in the UK and the US are too poor to access mainstream credit and banking services and are thereby excluded from a wide range of provisioning (Dymski 2007:9). Poor families often have to borrow from doorstep lenders at high, and sometimes extortionate, interest rates of up to 2,000 per cent (Pettifor 2003:25). Dymski cites the example of the pay day loan market, which in the US grew rapidly from the early 1990s. In 2001 it saw 70 million transactions (Dymski 2007:11). However, even pay day loans (borrowing until the next pay day) do not represent the most financially excluded, as borrowers need to have a checking account to be able to access the loans. In response to the demand for subprime credit, mainstream banks have increasingly linked up with subprime lenders.

While many households have been sucked into financialisation through high levels of debt, people have also been sucked in through the promise of profitable investment.

From Savings to Capital Investment

The financialisation of social life has seen people enticed into financialised capitalism through pensions and various forms of financial investments, including shares. This is characterised by an approach to savings that treats them more like capital, with the expectation of growth over time. As Langley has argued, there has been a shift to a market-oriented notion that pockets of money can be accumulated to secure individuals against the future. Security has become based on investment rather than insurance and collectivised risk (Langley 2006:920). The idea is that money or assets can be put aside so that welfare needs can be 'bought' in the market place rather than being available as social services when required. In a situation where money is rapidly entering the economy and asset prices are rising, this seems a reasonable option despite the fact that inflation more generally acts against all sorts of money-based saving such as pensions or trusts. The ideal is inflation in the investment market and stable prices in the consumer market. For a time the flood of money coming into the financial sector and the globalisation of production to minimise wage costs seemed to offer this ideal combination for the Anglo-American economies.

Pensions are an area where there has been a marked shift to the idea of investing in individualised wealth. Traditionally people had relied on their employer or the state to secure their pensions. In the 1970s the British Conservative government created incentives for people to opt out of work-based pension schemes and accumulate a 'personal pot' of savings and insurance. Many people were persuaded by commission-hungry salespeople to dump their company pension for a private one. This meant that they lost the employers' contribution to their pension and were also thrown on the mercy of the financial sector. Often these problems were not clearly explained, which resulted in a mis-selling scandal with pension companies being forced to pay compensation to around 5 million people. As with many financial investments, as money initially poured in returns looked very good, but as soon as the market turned, people faced an impoverished old age (Blackburn 2006). One mutual, Equitable Life, made the fatal mistake of guaranteeing a pension level to some of its savers which resulted in the collapse of the company as it became clear that such a promise was impossible to keep in fluctuating markets. Money purchase pensions also required huge 'pension pots' to create a reasonable pension income. In 2008 in Britain a pension pot of £100,000 would give an annual pension of under £5,000 a year and by 2009 this would be even lower as interest rates fell to 0.5 per cent. It is very unlikely that many people will have accumulated enough money in their private sector schemes to produce even this level of pension.

One of the claims for the democratisation of investment is the participation of many people in the stock market through institutional investors. In the US and UK before the crash, institutional investors held 40 per cent of the equity in the top 500 companies (Glyn 2007:55). However, Stanford argues that pensions cannot be the basis of a 'people's capitalism' as they have never formed a major part of share ownership, particularly in the US. Stanford claims US pension investments peaked at around 9 per cent in 1990 and had fallen to under 7 per cent by 2006. For

Britain the starting point was better, taking around 32 per cent of share investment in 1990, representing the strength of company pension schemes. However by 2006 this had collapsed to under 13 per cent (Stanford 2008:222). Investing in the stock market also had a very negative effect on pensions. Seeing the rising stock market value of their funds companies took pension holidays. They did not take account of the inevitable share falls as capitalism went through its business cycle. Firms did not secure their pension funds against difficult times and certainly did not put in enough to cover the possibility of share collapse. Royal Mail, BT and even the Bank of England had taken pension holidays. These left large holes in British pension funds totalling around £200 billion by 2008 and many funds shut their doors to new members or closed altogether. By 2009 very few defined benefit schemes were left where pensions were defined by length of employment or proportion of salary rather than economic performance.

The pension debacle is a good example of the total inappropriateness of a market approach to provisioning. It reveals a complete lack of economic wisdom and foresight on the part of major employers who did not anticipate the problems that would be created by the business cycle. It would be even worse if they knew full well what would happen when the stock market turned, but did not care. Even if they had been successful, occupational pension schemes only covered a minority of the population. Most people's only support in old age would be the state. Similarly, direct or indirect investment in the stock market was only open to a minority of the population. They are the 'fortunate 40 percent' of relatively wealthy households (Froud et al. 2001:72). This group has the majority of disposable income and accounts for 80 per cent of private and occupational pensions and their personalised savings directly accelerates inequality and privilege (Froud et al. 2001:76).

These people are the basis of what Lawson has referred to as the 'turbo consumer society' (2009:52). Lawson traces the turbo consumer society back to the ideas of the Austrians, Ludwig von Mises and Friedrich von Hayek. They argued against public expenditure in favour of private expenditure with a small state, low taxes and free markets which led to the whole panoply of privatisation and 'greed is good' (Lawson 2009:89). From the perspective of the investment winners the model seemed to hold good. According to Ann Pettifor, between 1982 and 2004 world average income rose only threefold whereas world financial assets increased in value 32 times: 'it turns out that working for a living over this period was most unrewarding. Earning rent on assets, by contrast, was immensely rewarding' (Pettifor 2006:80).

The privatised ideology of the financialised turbo consumer society encouraged people to join the private financial sector through the privatisation of public assets and the demutualisation of collective assets. During the rounds of privatizations under the British Conservative government in the 1980s people were encouraged to buy shares in previously publicly owned utilities such as telephones, gas and water. This resulted in many people joining the stock market for the first time. The privatisation policy initiated in the UK became a major aspect of neo-liberal policy around the world. People were encouraged to think of themselves as shareholders in the great capitalist bonanza, rather than members of mutual organisations or citizens. Britain had seen a major programme of nationalisation following World War II and had a long history of people engaging in structures of mutual financial support, such as friendly societies, insurance societies and building societies. Such organisations represented major solidaristic and collective innovation by working class people. Some had grown into large organisations such as the Halifax Building Society and the Trustee Savings Bank, both of which ended up as part of Lloyds Bank.

For the building societies, demutualisation was a response to competition from banks when credit restrictions were removed. Also, as building societies, they could not access the burgeoning money markets in the same way as banks. Following Abbey National's lead in 1988 others followed, some willingly, while others were driven by the activities of 'carpet baggers'. When building societies demutualised, in some cases members were issued with a block of shares regardless of how much they had invested. This meant that someone with £1,000 would get the same as someone with £100,000, usually a hundred or so shares. When these were traded on the stock market the owner got a windfall, in many cases much more than £1,000. This led to a tragic episode where people who probably had little care or interest in mutual societies spread their savings around several societies and led the pressure to demutualise, thereby making extensive windfall profits. As a result, the collective assets of more than a hundred years of working class savings passed to the capitalist financial sector. In the early 1970s there were over 150 building societies with total deposits of around £150 billion: by the end of 2008 there were only just over a third left. The remaining building societies tightened up their rules to prevent carpetbagging, but the damage had been done and working class savings were put at the mercy of the capitalist markets.

In 2007 the nationalisation of the former building society turned bank, Northern Rock, made clear the problem some people had distinguishing between share-holding and saving. 11 per cent of the shares were held by staff and more than 20 per cent by hedge funds, but the most vocal were the small shareholders, many of whom had retained the shares they had been allocated when the company converted from a building society. They saw these shares as 'savings' rather than 'investments' which could rise and fall. One woman interviewed in the media said she had lost her 'life savings'. Her shares had been worth £12,000 at their peak (£12 per share) but their value had now collapsed to a few hundred pounds at most. A spokesperson for the Northern Rock Small Shareholders Group said that nationalisation meant that the bank was being 'stolen' away from them. This left the government in a difficult position because it was being challenged to compensate shareholders for their losses. By 2008 all the privatised building societies had failed or had been absorbed by other banks. Following the banking crisis the remaining building societies saw their deposits rise dramatically as people returned to the safety of mutual savings.

Housing: Home or Asset?

Housing has been central to both the boom and the bust in the Anglo-American economies. Mortgage debt has been a major aspect of money creation in the second half of the twentieth century, accounting for up to 80 per cent of personal debt in the US and 60 per cent of bank loans (Phillips 2008:32). Financialisation of housing meant that homes were no longer seen as just places to live, but as a store of wealth. As house values rose, homes were seen as a kind of milch cow that could be milked for consumer spending or for life cycle costs such as college fees, health care needs or income in old age. House ownership was also a source of status, particularly in the UK and the US. Renting was seen as something poor people did, it was a waste of money as it did not accrue a financial asset. To have a mortgage was not a debt, but an investment.

Anglo-American 'home ownership ideology' is not universal. Spain and Greece, for example, have home ownership levels of over 80 per cent compared with 70 per cent in the UK and US and similar economies such as Australia, yet the latter have a much stronger link to market relations and neo-liberalism (Ronald 2008:2). Ronald's explanation is that much of the housing in economies such as Spain and Greece is rural and traditional with owner occupation linked to long term family residence. I can confirm from my own experience that rural property was once seen as having little or no value and could even be seen as a liability. My own family inherited cottages in a Cornish fishing village. In the 1950s they had no value as they were tumble down and without facilities. My father was trying to give them away. By the time of the crash those cottages were premium 'quaint' second homes changing hands for up to £400,000.

Ronald sees a commodified housing market as accompanying urbanisation and industrialisation. However, even in some urbanised societies, there is not such an ideological commitment to home-ownership. For example, in much of Europe there is very little stigma attached to rented housing (Ronald 2008:xi). Even public ownership is not necessarily a problem. In Singapore all housing is built and mortgaged by the state, with owner-occupied tenure for 99 years (Ronald 2008:6). One result of treating homes as financial assets is that British housing value is much higher in comparison to GDP than the European average. Based on 2005 figures, Ronald points out that housing equity in the EU is around 40 per cent of GDP whereas in the UK it is more than double GDP (£3.8 trillion to GDP £1.5 trillion) and housing debt is around one-third of GDP in Europe compared to 80 per cent in the UK (£800bn) (2008:3).

Home ownership in Britain and the US was strongly supported by government policy. Before World War I most people in Britain rented privately, but by the end of the century the position was largely reversed with the majority being owner-occupiers. Support was provided through government support for expanded building society activity, municipal mortgages and mortgage tax relief, although from the 1970s the latter was reduced and then abolished. In the US home ownership was actively encouraged and underwritten by the state through the home loan organisations Fannie Mae and then Freddie Mac. Fannie Mae, the Federal National Mortgage Agency, was created by the Roosevelt government to provide mortgage funds following the Depression, and Freddie Mac, the Federal Home Mortgage Corporation, was created in 1970 to provide competition for Fannie Mae. Mortgages were long term and fixed rate. The Labour Party in Britain did promote public sector housing which rose to around 30 per cent of total housing by the 1970s. However, successive Conservative governments raised the cost of public housing substantially, and encouraged tenants to buy their council houses with deep discounts. As a result, more than 2 million homes transferred to the private sector. House building by local authorities also effectively ceased and restrictions were put on municipal mortgages. Local public housing was replaced by social housing built through housing associations and funded by a national body, the Housing Corporation.

The collapsing housing market in the US and the UK in 2006–07 marked the end of a remarkable era when home ownership had been a key aspect of most people's lives and expectations. Much of this was related to the incredible boom in house prices that made housing an important area of speculative growth and capital accumulation for buyers, builders and lenders. House prices in Britain had been rising since the early 1970s and particularly at the end of the 1980s before they fell back during 1988–92. Prices started to rise again rapidly from 1995 and particularly from 2000 in a huge bubble of house price inflation that followed the end of the dotcom boom. As prices rose people were able to raise more debts on the increased value of their housing through 'equity release'. Applying the concept of equity release to taking a second mortgage or trading down the housing market to release value indicates the way this growth in value was perceived. Rather than being seen as house price inflation, or evidence of an unsustainable boom, house-owners were encouraged to see these gains as permanent, even though the period from 1988 to 1992 in Britain was recent evidence that house prices could fall sharply.

Rising house prices, or more correctly house price inflation, encouraged the view of homes as assets. Housing had become monetised or 'propertized' (Ronald 2008:112). The housing market seemed to be able to create wealth out of nowhere which, given the huge shift to bank-based credit money creation, is exactly what it was doing. House price inflation created ideological support for financialisation, capital accumulation and the capitalist market system. Middle England didn't seem to mind the rich getting markedly richer and the number of billionaires increasing, when annual house price rises could be higher than annual wages, which were generally stagnant or falling in real terms. Treating housing as a rising and secure financial asset also allowed neo-liberal policy makers to encourage the idea of asset-based welfare; that is, the house can be seen as a source of money for the future when needed. As Ronald argues, 'Whether or not owner-occupied homes can effectively provide insurance against the risks of economic conditions is highly questionable, and they may constitute greater exposure to risk...what is constructed as security, opportunity and choice...is essentially risk' (2008:109). This is particularly the case where people were encouraged to 'release equity' which actually meant taking out a loan and putting their house at risk if they could not pay, or ceding their home to a finance company in return for cash or an income. An asset-based welfare system with its promises of opportunity and choice will inevitably be undermined if asset prices start to drop. There is also a conflict in seeing a house as an asset for personal security and as an asset for family wealth. Homeowners may not, in practice, be happy to see their homes sold to pay for care in old age, instead of being passed on to their children as an inheritance.

Engagement with financial markets also had further manifestations within the housing sector. In Britain one was the formal linking of mortgages to the stock market through so-called endowment mortgages. These were launched in the 1980s. Interest was paid to the mortgage company, but the capital sum of the loan was invested in the stock market. These mortgages were slightly cheaper than traditional repayment mortgages and were sold aggressively. At their peak up to 80 per cent of UK mortgages were endowment-based. This very large swing of money to the stock market could arguably explain the long stock market boom. As is usual in new markets, the first people to take out these mortgages made a lot of money but as the market peaked those last in were left with deficits. Houses were also bought directly as financial assets through 'buy-to-let'. This resulted in an expansion of the private rented sector, with many of the new tenants being people who could not afford to buy houses. The UK Council of Mortgage Lenders reported in 2006 that 750,000 buy-to-let mortgages had been granted since 1996. The buy-to-let market was helped by the fact that from 1996 people had been able to buy with interest-only mortgages, coupled with very low interest rates. For one building society turned bank, Bradford and Bingley, buy-to-lets accounted for up to a half of its mortgage book with securitisation providing a similar proportion of its funding. This contributed to its collapse in 2008. Similar problems were experienced by other building societies including the West Bromwich and the Dunfermline. The speculation in buy-to-let, together with large scale building, particularly of inner city flats, led to many buy-to-let owners facing severe deficits and repossession. Often tenants, through no fault of their own, found themselves evicted at short notice when owners defaulted.

One of the main triggers of the financial crisis was lending to subprime borrowers. Subprime borrowers are those without a credit record, with a bad credit record or no deposit and low, insecure income or even no income. With so much cheap money sloshing around the money markets and the boom in house prices, even very marginal people began to look profitable, particularly as they could be charged higher rates of interest. Potential homeowners, or those with low, or no, debt on their homes, were often seduced by promises of low interest rates, although the small print said that rate would only prevail for a short time, sometimes only a month or even a day. People were able to self-certificate their earnings. Earnings were often exaggerated, either by the borrower or the salesperson drawing up the contract. Some loans were described as 'NINJA' loans – no income, no job, no assets. House buyers in the US were particularly vulnerable to sales pressure because they often did not understand the new forms of mortgage on offer. They had been accustomed to fixed rate mortgages for 30 years and many were sitting on houses with a high capital value. They were faced with tempting sounding options that would 'release capital' from their homes or allow them to become homeowners for the first time. They were offered adjustable rate loans rather than the fixed rate they were used to, piggyback loans, short term teaser rates, low interest or interest-only mortgages that appeared to be within borrowers' means, but with no mechanism for repayment or analysis of future capacity to pay. Rather cynically, some of these were christened 'neutron' loans which, like neutron bombs, were designed to impact on people without damaging the economic viability of property. With interest rates very low and existing financial institutions finding it difficult to make a profit, even well known high street banks entered the subprime market.

Until things went very wrong, subprime lending was seen as helping disadvantaged groups to access the housing market. The African-American community, in particular, was excluded from commercial and government sponsored mainstream mortgage finance through 'redlining', that is, areas where loans were not made as they were thought to be more risky. From the late 1960s onwards a series of reforms aimed to end redlining including the 1968 Fair Housing Act, 1974 Equal Credit Opportunity Act, Home Mortgage Disclosure Act 1975 and Community Reinvestment Act of 1977 (Dymski 2007:8). Because of this history of discrimination, the US government did nothing to halt the growth in subprime lending, and even encouraged it, as it seemed to be offering the chance of home ownership to the excluded poor. The 1977 Community Reinvestment Act had put the onus on US banks to provide financial services to poor communities. President Clinton used this legislation to urge banks to expand their lending to financially excluded groups. This took subprime loans from 5 per cent of the total in 1998 to 30 per cent of the total by 2007. Interest-only mortgages became very prevalent towards the end of the housing boom. As these mortgages did not necessarily have any mechanism to repay the capital, they were arguably much worse for the holder than renting. Scurlock reports that by 2007 half of new mortgages in California were interest-only; in the UK at least 30 per cent were interest-only (2007:38). Not all the subprime loans were what they seemed. Dymski quotes a study that showed that many of those acquiring subprime mortgages in the US should have been eligible for a conventional loan: up to 51 per cent in 2005 and up to 61 per cent in 2006 (Dymski 2007:15). However, by this stage the commercial benefit of making subprime loans outweighed any concern for the economic status of the people concerned.

In the UK one of the most active banks in the field of 'democratised' lending was Northern Rock, which provided mortgages for people who were trying to enter the housing market for the first time (Walters 2008:33). It lent to people who did not have deposits and would lend up to six times income. There was general recognition that young people were finding it hard to get on the property ladder and Northern Rock was seen as a bank that would help them do so. It was also willing to lend more than the value of the house through its 'Together' loans that allowed people to borrow 125 per cent of the value of a property. This meant the bank was very exposed to non-payment or to a fall in house prices. It was also very exposed to securitisation which led to its collapse in September 2007 (Brummer 2008:7). The subprime crisis heralded that the dream was over and by 2009 one in nine UK mortgage-holders were thought to be in negative equity. House prices had fallen substantially and the housing market had stalled. The US market had also collapsed with price drops of up to 50 per cent with forecasts of foreclosures of between 1 and 2 million. Phillips sees the cost of the housing crash in the US as reaching $10 trillion, about half of total housing market value, with major parallels to the 1930s housing crash, when 10 per cent of homes foreclosed (2008:12).

One of the many negative aspects of the financialisation of housing was the failure to see it as an inflationary boom. While it lasted, the rapidly rising prices resulted in a massive transfer of wealth between the generations. The older generation who had benefitted from the rising price of property during the boom years were selling to the young who were having to pay for that wealth through their own debt. Many young people were priced out of the housing market, but those who did buy were mortgaging themselves very heavily, sometimes up to seven times household income. Equally, those who were 'releasing' the value of their homes with new mortgages were taking on more debt. The wealth that had been wrapped up in housing was being sold via securitised equity release and new mortgage vehicles. The accumulated value of generations was being turned back into debt, while the assets themselves tumbled in price. It remains to be seen what the economic hangover of this financial binge will be. Whatever the outcome, debt will be an important aspect. As Scurlock puts it, homes were a 'debt-delivery mechanism' (2007:33) where, until the crash, Americans were 'making money selling each other houses with money borrowed from the Chinese' (2007:27). The money borrowed from the Chinese was, in fact, recycled dollars from the US balance of payments deficit. Through its cheap labour and trading dominance China was accumulating large amounts of dollars which it returned to the US mainly by buying US government debt and helping to keep interest rates low.

While it would not be correct to blame the Chinese for the ills of American financial capitalism, certainly in a boom people do make money, quite literally through borrowing, and that is why booms are so very hard to stop as no-one wants to spoil the party.

Debt as Development

While mortgages were a major source of debt-based money issue in the latter half of the twentieth century, debt was also being seen as an instrument of social policy. Given that debt has been so central to the development of modern economies, it is not surprising that debt should be seen as an agent of economic development. Hernando de Soto has long promoted the idea of granting property rights to poor households so that they have assets against which to raise credit at a reasonable price (2000:24). As a policy instrument, the use of debt to enhance development gained its most public profile through the work of Mohammad Yunus and the idea of microcredit.

In 1976, Mohammad Yunus gave small loans to buy working materials to some craftworkers in Bangladesh who were being forced to borrow small sums from traders and money lenders at extortionate rates. Yunus's loans substantially improved the economic viability of the borrowers and the loans were readily repaid. This led to the founding of the Grameen Bank in 1982. By 1998 it had over a thousand branches employing around 12,000 people lending to more than 2 million borrowers. Loan defaults were very low initially at around 2 per cent but rose somewhat over time (Affleck and Mellor 2003:33). The principles of microcredit are that loans are very small and borrowers are not required to demonstrate prior possession of savings or collateral. In fact, loans are targeted at those who do not have assets or banking access. Under the Grameen principle, borrowers are brought together in small groups and collectively guarantee repayment. This puts considerable peer pressure on individual borrowers and also has the effect of putting the risk and costs of default on to the borrowers themselves. Interest rates are quite high for borrowers, although still much lower than money-lender rates. This is because the loans have to cover administration and training costs which are high in relation to the small sums being handed out. Yunus was awarded the Nobel Peace Prize in 2006 and his movement has spread even to the heart of capitalism in New York City, where a branch has been set up in a low-income area to counter the explosive growth of expensive payday loan companies, cheque cashers and pawn shops. Microcredit became an important aspect of development programmes with a microcredit summit held in Washington DC in 1997 and the General Assembly of the UN declaring 2005 the International Year of Microcredit.

Unlike 'top down' development projects, microcredit was seen as a 'bottom up' approach enabling people to escape permanently from the bondage of poverty by achieving social change through economic empowerment. It was to be a market solution to poverty (Affleck and Mellor 2006:309). Microcredit would tap the potential for entrepreneurship that was assumed to lie within the community itself. The main barrier was seen as lack of financial access. The market was ready and waiting, all that was missing was some financial credit and business training. Through microcredit people, particularly women, were encouraged to borrow and invest their way out of poverty. Its supporters claim that many millions of people have been helped and that local economies can be invigorated by small scale injections of cash and people can be empowered by taking control of their own livelihoods. By December 2002 there were nearly 70 million clients linked to over 3,000 microcredit organisations and around two-thirds of the borrowers were women (Fernando 2006:1). The centrality of women borrowers is a very notable feature of the microcredit movement, although there is debate about whether it achieves women's economic empowerment (Pearson 2001:312).

Some commentators argue that the good intentions of the microcredit movement are distorted in practice by the wider framework of financial drivers. As the microcredit approach to development has become more mainstream, it is losing its local and personal focus. As Fisher and Sriram argue, microcredit has tended to become a top down policy, seen as an end in itself rather than a means to other more socially-based development approaches. They subtitle their book 'putting development back into microfinance' (2002). Fernando, in his study of microcredit in Bangladesh and Sri Lanka, also noted that a large number of mainstream banks were entering the field, indicating that microfinance was moving up market with less concern for the very poor. Fernando also notes the pressure that funders were putting on NGOs to show early results from microcredit initiatives. Ensuring success meant excluding the poorest and putting pressure on borrowers: 'the so-called collateral-free lending practices of the NGOs not only exclude the poorest of the poor but, even more strikingly, also function as mechanisms of controlling and disciplining the lives of the borrowers' (Fernando 2006:26). Borrowers were often expected to start repayments immediately, rather than allowing enterprises to grow. Overemphasis on microfinance also led some NGOs virtually to become banks.

Fernando fears that notions of bottom up self-help could mask the withdrawal of state responsibility for the needs of the poor: 'the language of reliance, self sufficiency and empowerment through microfinance appear to be extremely productive given that they simultaneously provide legitimacy for the withdrawal of the state from development, and creates conditions for capitalist expansion' (2006:21). Fernando points out that at present 80 per cent of the world's population live mainly within the informal sector without access to finance. If through judicious use of credit these people could be encouraged to create their own economic dynamism, this would have a range of benefits for capitalism. As well as making up for the lack of a welfare state, or the problems of the wider economy, it would help support underpaid workers and, in the longer run, provide new markets (Fernando 2006:17–18).

The main challenge is whether finance through debt can achieve economic development for poorer communities. One of the main aims of microcredit is to create microenterprises that would eventually be able to access mainstream bank credit and grow into larger enterprises that could build a local economy. Margolis suggests that microcredit is not economically feasible for the very poor, and points out that the Brazilian government has had to pick up nearly half the lenders' costs for a credit programme covering

1.3 million subsistence farmers (Margolis 2007). Another problem is that there may not be the level of untapped entrepreneurship that the microcredit approach would hope. Evidence from interviews with micro-lenders in the UK indicate that making credit available is unlikely to stimulate widespread economic activity, in fact many lenders were having trouble getting their money 'out of the doors' (Affleck and Mellor 2006:314). As an earlier study of the formation of worker co-operatives in the face of factory closure indicated, it is very hard for people to enter a market that has already excluded them (Mellor et al. 1988:79). It increases economic pressures on those who are already marginalised within the wider economic community if they also have to take on debt. Debt-free credit might be more successful, but this is not what is on offer within market oriented microcredit: it is credit as debt. A more promising aspect of the microfinance movement is to provide funding for social enterprises (Pearce 2003:106). These are organisations founded on democratic principles that trade for social benefit. Such organisations cannot be judged by market tests of viability. They are set up to serve poor communities and the most appropriate form of funding would be a grant or interest-free loan, or a combination of both.

Debt and Capitalism

The rising level of debt has been central to economic growth within the UK and US economies, particularly the expansion of personal and mortgage debt. Phillips calculates that, before its collapse, the US housing sector and its services, with $12 trillion of mortgage debt, represented 25 per cent of GDP and 40 per cent of US growth (Phillips 2008:11). Equity release through refinanced mortgages alone accounted for 20 per cent of US growth in 2002, while in the UK households took out the equivalent of $19 billion worth of refinanced mortgages in the third quarter of 2002 alone (Harvey 2003:112–13). Lawson argues that house prices drove the UK consumer boom with £246 billion of equity wealth being withdrawn from housing in the ten years to 2009 (Lawson 2009:83). By the latter part of the twentieth century, debt had become an important element in sustaining household expenditure in the face of stagnating incomes (Panitch and Konings 2009:72). In the short term, together with globalised cheap labour goods, this appeared to overcome Marx's prediction that capitalism would be in crisis if the mass of the people in society did not receive enough in wages to enable them to buy the products of the economy. However, the danger in relying on debt to maintain the dynamics of the economy is that it depends on people's willingness, or ability, to take on debt and, as later became apparent, the willingness of banks to make loans. As Harvey has argued, 'ever expanding endebtedness is a perilous way to keep consumerism alive' (Harvey 2003:77).

Writing in the *Guardian* newspaper in 2003, Wynne Godley and Alex Izurieta argued that the only driving force for the British economy since 1997 had been household expenditure (and household debt) with the ratio of debt to income rising to 120 per cent by 2002–03 (22 July 2003). Phillips describes Anglo-Saxon speculative capitalism as being an orgy of credit and debt with governments and economists turning a blind eye to the dangerous growth in private debt. In 2007 US private (financial, personal, mortgage and corporate) debt was $37 trillion as opposed to government debt (federal, state and local) of $11 trillion. This total of $48 trillion had grown from $10.5 trillion in 1987. Phillips notes that this is three times larger than US GDP and is very similar in ratio to the position in 1929 when debt was 287 per cent of GDP (2008:181). Even so, debt generated growth was reaching its limit: in the US by September 2003 it was taking six dollars of extra debt to generate one dollar of growth.

The dilemma for the financialised Anglo-American economies was that debt had become a (failing) agent of growth and a heavy burden to borrowers. Elastic debt issue may have enabled capitalism to expand, but it has severe limitations as a solution to poverty and has led to immense inequality. As Smithin has argued against de Soto's case for property title and access to credit as a source of future wealth, capacity for earning money is also important (Smithin 2009:63). When the only source of future income is more debt being issued, it cannot be a secure source of wealth. Japan is a clear example of the limits of debt-based growth with its seemingly unmovable debt overhang (Krugman 2008:56). While bank issue of debt money has been central to the growth of capitalism, it has its own limits and contradictions. When debt issue becomes the only engine of capitalist growth it must eventually come up against Marx's contradiction that, if profit is to be extracted, people will not have sufficient money to enable them to consume all the goods produced, even with debt. The debt machine must run out of steam.

Conclusion

A substantial minority of people have become entangled with the financial system in many ways. They have become heavily involved in financial investments through pension funds and other sorts of invested savings. At first these investments made the capitalist system seem like a horn of plenty as they tapped new sources of money. The privatisation of public utilities and conversion of mutual societies to private companies also produced a new generation of shareholders. As a result, a large number of people have experienced the roller coaster of capitalist boom and slump. They have also become involved, actively or passively, in asset price inflation, mainly through housing. While some people have treated housing as a capital investment, many others have more passively experienced house prices rises and therefore have shared the expectation that they, or their family, will benefit from a highly valued home. If house prices collapse, as some people predict, by between 40 and 50 per cent in real terms over time, these expectations stand to be disappointed. At the same time many families, rich and poor, are facing unprecedented levels of debt. Governments are struggling to get lending going, but it may be that people have reached their absolute limits. There is no growth left within the household sector and as this has largely driven the booms, there is nowhere to go.

The full economic and political consequences of the Anglo-American experiment in financialising private life remains to be seen. The Great Depression in the 1930s in the US and UK brought about radical change towards the left. In Germany, economic collapse brought fascism. The difference may well depend upon which politicians and leaders seize the moment. There is a danger that the collapse of the economy together with the collapse of the dreams of people caught up in it, will lead to a profound distrust of the economic and political process. The capacity of democratic leaders to respond to this disillusionment will depend upon the extent to which they understand the underlying problems of the economy, in particular the vital role played by the capitalist capture of the issue and circulation of money. This will be discussed in the next chapter.

rang up Philip Booth
to get transcript of
Glasman's talk.

4

CREDIT AND CAPITALISM

As previous chapters have shown, credit is essential to contemporary capitalism. This is for three reasons. The first reason would be common to all businesses whether capitalist or not. Money is needed to enable the productive or trading process to start. Producers need to purchase raw materials, machinery and labour to create products before they can be sold. Traders need money to buy goods to trade before they can sell them to customers. For small traders this money may be provided by family members, but even that money must also have been issued at some point. Money has to come into being whether as tangible currency such as coins or beads, or as less tangible credit. A trader may get goods from a producer on credit pending sale. The credit notes that traders issued formed one of the origins of the modern banking system. The case made in Chapter 1 is that money does not emerge from a prior exchange of goods: the issue of money as credit is the start of the production and exchange process. Banks have played a major part in the issue of money as credit, that is, as debt to the borrower.

The second reason is that while producers and traders need credit to start the economic process, customers also need credit to be able to purchase goods. This is either because the goods are too expensive for cash payment such as a house or a car, or people do not have enough money to buy the goods produced. Running up debts to enable consumption goes back a very long way. Inheritors of feudal property rapidly converted this into cash by taking out mortgages, quite literally a debt until death (Rowbotham 1998:31). More recently, and more specific to capitalism, consumers have needed to borrow to maintain consumption because they do not earn enough to purchase the goods produced. This is the classic dilemma for capitalism that Marx identified. Workers' wages are much less than the value of the goods they produce. The difference, the surplus value created, contributes to the profit of the business. The problem comes when those goods come to market and there is not enough money circulating through wages to enable people to buy all the goods. If another market cannot be found, the surplus value cannot be 'realised' through the sale of all the goods. Enabling the consumer to access credit whether through hire purchase, deferred payment, personal credit or second mortgages on homes bridges the gap and enables the purchase of all the goods on offer. This does not solve the basic problem: it defers it until people become so indebted that they cannot afford any more credit.

The third reason is the most important for capitalism. If capital is to accumulate there must always be new money coming into the system. Capitalism must expand or die. This is because of the way capitalism functions and the role of money in enabling profit to be extracted from the circuit of production and exchange. Marx made a clear distinction between commodity exchange through markets and capitalist exchange. As discussed in Chapter 1, in commodity exchange money is the medium which enables goods to be offered for sale and purchased. A commodity is sold for money and the money is then used to buy another commodity $(C - M - C)$. Capitalism is very different. The motive for making the commodity in the first place is to make money. Money is therefore invested in commodity production with the aim of selling that commodity at a profit, that is, $M - C - M+$. Whereas the first system could operate on a steady state basis without necessarily dramatically expanding the money supply, the second must have a continually growing supply of money to create the desired profit. The desire to extract more money than is put in to the process through wages and other costs is a dilemma for capitalism. Within the circuit of production and exchange, more money must come from somewhere if profit is to be made and capital is to accumulate. Therefore to make this circuit possible new money must continually enter the system.

For this reason, the way money is issued as credit in a capitalist economy cannot rely on obtaining credit from prior savings as this is not new money. Therefore lending, as discussed in Chapter 2, cannot be related to some previous stock of money issued, but must reflect a bank's willingness to create liquidity, that is, to create more money. While it may be possible for one capitalist to extract more money from the economy than was put in during production (as wages, cost of raw materials etc.), this cannot be done for the economy as a whole. As Smithin points out, for capitalism to survive it must require someone to hold a deficit, that is, go into debt. Debt is therefore central to capitalism. Money profits are enabled by money creation over and above the initial costs of production: 'in capitalism, the creation of credit is…an integral part of the productive system…the realisation of profit' (Smithin 2009:12). Finance, and particularly credit, has been central to the growth of the capitalist system. Access to money or credit is the most 'relevant source of power in the capitalist system' (Smithin 2009:72).

From Finance Capital to Financialisation

A key stage in the emergence of capitalism was the shift from physical ownership to financial ownership. Veblen (1899) and Hilferding (1910/1985) both saw the emergence of paper claims to productive capacity, that is, the stock market, as a new stage in capitalist development from productive capitalism to finance capitalism. Paper ownership of productive facilities allowed absentee ownership of productive resources, but it also allowed capital to accumulate through the buying and selling of shares. However, the paper ownership was not the real source of wealth. Paper ownership was 'fictitious' in the sense that wealth came from the real productive sources that the paper represented. The main difference between a traditional Marxist approach to finance capital and the new financialised regime is that financial assets are no longer seen as 'fictitious'. In the traditional theory of finance capital the pieces of paper that were traded through the stock market represented real factories and businesses. The paper had no value in itself. Financialisation sees financial assets not as representing wealth in the 'real' economy, but as wealth creating investments in their own right (Wigan 2009). In the new financial era 'there is no necessary connection between productive investment and the amassing of financial assets' (Foster and Magdoff 2009:82).

The new era of capitalist finance turned the money system into an object of capitalist speculation. Money itself became something to be traded as currency controls were removed. Daily foreign exchange transactions moved from $570 billion in 1989 to $1.9 trillion by 2004 (Epstein 2005:4).The financial sector no longer serviced the wider economy: it had become the economy, particularly in the US and the UK. Within companies financialisation led to the dominance of financial gains and the rise in importance of shareholder value, in the banks as much as elsewhere. As they were growing very quickly, banks became stars of the new financialised world and their share price rose rapidly. Financialisation also drove the growth of the money markets which fed into the new ways of raising and circulating money. The preoccupations and needs of the financial markets began to dominate the rest of the economy. The strength of the new market in money rested on a stream of liquidity (Langley 2010). 'Leverage' became an important aspect of financial investment, that is, speculation with borrowed money or speculation based on partial payment of a financial asset (bought 'on the margin'). Financialisation and the new money markets seemed to have the Midas touch and this gave rise to the notion of a 'turbo-capitalism' that seemed to be able to produce unlimited wealth. The market could do no wrong and participants in the financial sector were lauded and showered with financial rewards.

Financialised capitalism is a stage where money is invested in financial assets to create more money (M – M – M+). By 2000 UK money supply was growing more than twice as fast as GDP (Scott Cato 2009:79). Financial gain becomes the only measure of successful economic action, summed up in concepts such as the bottom line and shareholder value. The money value of an object, asset or activity is much more important than its use or beauty. The drive towards the financial sector and prioritising shareholder or investor value rather than value to the employee, customer or wider society, was not solely driven by accumulation strategies for finance capitalism. The financialisation of everyday life (Langley 2008:49) meant that pensions increasingly relied on funding through financial growth and many people had been seduced into seeing savings as investments. Growth in the financial sector eclipsed other sectors of the economy. Financial firms and financial assets were much more profitable than traditional production and exchange. Profits of the US financial sector went from 20 per cent of non-financial profits in the 1980s to 50 per cent in 2000 (Glyn 2007:52). With little profit to be made in manufacturing, even traditional industries turned to investment in financial services. In 2004 40 per cent of corporate profits in the US came from financial activities and only 10 per cent from manufacturing (Phillips 2008:26). By 2008 there were two dollars invested in financial assets as against one dollar in 'tangible capital' (Stanford 2008:219).

State support was vital to the dominance of the financial sectors in the US and UK. In 1980s Thatcher's Britain, as in Reagan's America, the financial sector rose to social and economic prominence while the productive sector was run down, particularly in industries where trades unions were strong. Factories in Britain were dismantled and their assembly lines sometimes taken abroad. Basic industries such as mining were closed down as uneconomic. The stock market was no longer an engine for raising money for the productive sector, but a forum for speculation. In the US more than 95 per cent of its activities were speculating and trading in already-issued equity: the buying and selling of existing shares (Stanford 2008:218). If companies wanted to raise money they were more likely to go to a bank or raise money directly on the money markets by issuing a bond. Rather than resist finan-cialisation, the US and UK governments aimed to ride the new beast. They sought to be market leaders in global finance. Both governments deregulated the financial sector, a policy continued by the Democrats and New Labour. 'Light touch' regulation was promoted despite a history of regular financial crises on a national and international scale, including the secondary banking scandals of the 1970s, the Third World debt crisis, the Latin American crisis, the Asian crisis, the Savings and Loans problem in the US and many others.

While there was certainly ideological pressure for deregulation from the free market lobby, it was also clear that governments were acceding to the realities of globalised finance capital as it escaped from national control. Financialisation, neo-liberalism and globalisation were driving the policy agenda with governments trailing in their wake. Saul sees the development of the globalised market system, and the ideology of progress by private economic development alone, as beginning with the final collapse of the Bretton Woods framework for global finance in the early 1970s (2005:55). Market fundamentalism then established its ideological and practical dominance through the deregulation of financial systems, privatisation of public assets and the formation of bodies to promote market ideology such as the World Trade Organisation. The financial market was seen as particularly efficient in distributing money to the most profitable investments. It was even claimed that the operation of the international financial market would smooth out the problem of volatile currencies, in effect replace the Gold Standard (Bryan and Rafferty 2007:32). Speculators would seek out undervalued or overvalued currencies and buy or sell them until they reached the 'correct' level. George Soros was an early exemplar when he speculated through his Quantum investment fund against the British pound in 1992 leading Britain to pull out of the European Exchange Rate Mechanism.

The political dominance of capitalist finance enabled the emergence of a new layer of super-rich individuals which led one British commentator to ask 'who runs Britain?' (Peston 2008). As Peston points out, the sums of money earned by 'uber-capitalists' particularly in the financial sector are 'absurdly large' enabling the creation of 'well-heeled dynasties that have not been seen since Victorian times' (Peston 2008:14). Other writers have seen the markets as being revered almost as religions, for example Larry Elliott and Dan Atkinson's 'The Gods that Failed' (2008) and

Thomas Franks' 'One Market under God' (2001). The dominance of finance in the late twentieth century was represented by dynamic images of finance and speculation. Most of the new recruits were young males who were often pictured on the news or in fiction shouting into phones in shirt sleeves. Greed was good. Huge salaries and bonuses rewarded short-term profits, based on share price and turnover, rather than rewarding long-term stewardship. The whole of the City was permeated by a bonus culture where annual pay of £20 million or even £40 million was not deemed excessive. Corporate expenditure and hospitality was extensive. John Thain, the ex-CEO of Merrill Lynch, which had had to be rescued by Bank of America, reportedly had managed to spend a million dollars just refitting his office.

Earnings in hedge funds and private equity companies were even higher. Four of the top hedge fund chiefs including George Soros were reputed to have earned over $1 billion in 2008. Finance-driven wealth was not limited to finance companies. Stock options and other incentives to maximise shareholder value led the CEOs of the top 500 US companies to move from 30 times worker earnings in 1970 to 570 times in 2000. This compared with only 10–25 times in Japan and Europe (Glyn 2007:58). Unlike the sweatshop workers of the old productive industries, there seemed to be no losers in this new breed of capitalism. As the stock market rose and profits increased, so did the income of pension funds and other investments in financial assets. Inequality was growing rapidly with an increasingly impoverished minority being left behind, but finance capitalism seemed to be able to claim the moral high ground, or at least the political high ground. The financial sector also seemed to have the secret of magical money making with its opaque science of algorithmic trading developed by the so-called 'rocket scientists', an alchemy not available to ordinary mortals. One UK financial company even called itself Alchemy.

Deregulation, and the repeal of laws that separated utility banking from investment banking, meant that capitalism was once more able to exploit the speculative benefits of access to virtually unlimited credit creation. Leverage became the most important tool of financial accumulation. Leverage is just another word for debt, but it is the way that the debt is used that is important. In the same way that pressure on a small lever can move a large boulder, debt piled on a small amount of initial investment can vastly increase the profit made. The secret is access to cheap credit, borrowed in the short term to make the trade, and banks were lending incredibly cheaply to speculative finance companies. As Lowenstein records, the failed hedge fund Long Term Capital Management (LTCM) was able to access large amounts of very cheap credit with virtually no questions asked (2001:82). Highly leveraged investment enabled rapid capital accumulation, particularly in the activities of hedge funds, private equity companies and the privatisation of public assets.

Credit and Speculation: Hedge Funds and Derivatives

Hedge funds are mainly private companies that invest money for wealthy individuals. Phillips describes them as 'betting syndicates for the very rich' and estimates that at their height, hedge fund activities accounted for up to half of daily trading on the London and New York stock exchanges (2008:6). Hedge fund assets are often held offshore and investment is usually a minimum of a million dollars. Fund managers charge fees of between 1 and 2 per cent and take 20 per cent of the profits. Their earnings are often in excess of $250 million. In January 2007, in the run up to the crisis, there were more than 10,000 hedge funds with a reported $2.1 trillion in assets (Peston 2008:178). They became a major source of income for investment banks, even in Europe. In 2007 26 per cent of the revenues of the big European banks came from hedge funds (Veneroso 2008).

Access to bank credit is central to financial accumulation in hedge funds, even though their investors are already very rich people. Leverage greatly enhances the profitability of hedge activities and can go up to 40:1 or more (ratio of borrowing to investment). The principle is simple. If £100 was invested in a stock market or currency gamble which would bring a return of 2 per cent that would bring a total return of £102. If however a short term loan of £1,000 at a cost of 1 per cent was added that would make an additional £20 profit, less £10 in interest. The original sum of £100 would now make £112, a much better return. The lending bank would have earned a substantial fee for a very short term loan. If investors leverage up their bets and win, they pocket money made not only by their own invested money, but by the privately created resource of credit money. Profits on some hedge funds were up to 100 per cent or more, indicating that the benefit of using leverage was enormous.

A major activity of hedge funds is derivative trading. This is where productive or financial assets are not traded directly but at one remove: in effect, a bet on a future market movement. The simplest example is a 'future' such as a farmer agreeing to sell a crop after the harvest for a particular price. A more complex example would be an international trader agreeing a price in another currency for delivery in six months time and then insuring that price with another company, or agreeing to buy that currency at a particular price in the future to make sure that any change in currency values would not affect income at the point of sale. The usefulness of these types of activities makes it very difficult for governments to ban hedging activities outright. However, most hedge fund derivative activities are purely speculative, that is, there is no underlying exchange of goods or services. They gamble on anything, shares, securities, futures, currencies. Although the idea of hedging had been around for some time, the real growth in hedge funds stemmed from the 1970s when exchange rates were floated after the Bretton Woods system finally broke down and the dollar was no longer pegged to a nominal value in gold. The activities of hedge funds can have a major impact in world currency markets. It has been estimated that speculation could account for up to 95 per cent of daily international currency movements (Stretton 1999:720). George Soros's Quantum Fund bid against sterling in 1992 made his fund $1 billion profit in one day.

The huge growth in hedge funds was enabled by the work of Fischer Black, Robert Merton and Myron S. Scholes. In the 1970s they developed what has become known as the Black–Scholes model for pricing options, for which Merton and Scholes were awarded the Nobel Prize in 1997 (Fischer Black had died before the prize was awarded). The Black–Scholes model is a formula that enables computerised portfolios of investments in complex hedging arrangements. This quantitative or algorithmic method enabled fund managers to set up patterns of derivatives that off-set each other so that (theoretically) every possibility was covered. It was argued that such calculations enabled risk to be anticipated and priced. The people who undertook this modelling were described as 'rocket scientists' as many had science or maths degrees. The claim was that the model was so comprehensive in guarding against all outcomes that investments using its formula were fail-safe.

One of the attractions of hedge funds to investors is that they can make money in a rising or a falling market. In a rising market they can invest 'long', that is buy a share or other financial asset at a low price, hoping to sell at a higher price on a later date. In a falling market they can go 'short', that is, selling an asset they do not at that point own, hoping that prices will fall. Sometimes the asset sold is borrowed from another owner for a fee. This is then sold and the investor/gambler hopes to buy replacement assets at a later date at a cheaper price. Sometimes the investor goes 'naked', that is, they do not have an asset to sell at all. If too many investors promise to sell what they do not have, there may be no assets available to buy when the time comes to hand over the asset. Another way of engaging in speculation on credit is to trade 'on the margin'. This is effectively leveraging without borrowing money. The speculator pays part of the price of the asset, intending to pay the full amount after the trade. Equally, a small sum may be put down in order to secure the option of buying or selling something in the future. If all goes well, a lot of money is made for very little outlay. If all goes badly, the real value of the trade may have to be found.

One of the more outrageous ways in which banks can be embroiled in hedge fund activities is where no actual options were bought or sold but the fund took a 'position' or side-bet with a bank. For a fee, the bank would reimburse the speculator with the profit they would have made if the 'investment' was successful, that is, if the actual price of the stock or security moved in the right direction. This is directly equivalent to gambling, with the bank acting like a bookmaker in the casino of capitalism (Strange 1986). Because they are seen as private investment organisations, hedge funds are not regulated by the central bank or stock market regulators and do not need to be transparent in their dealings. This has led to suspicions about their activities and some of the risks they take. Derivatives in particular have famously been described by the world's richest man, Warren Buffet, as financial weapons of mass destruction. The case made by regulators such as Alan Greenspan is that because hedge funds use their own money they are not of concern to the regulators. This is certainly not the case if hedge funds are leveraging by borrowing from regulated banks or, as with Bear Stearns, need rescuing by the state while leveraging at 40:1 (Veneroso 2008).

The general acceptance of the proliferation of hedge funds, with their lack of transparency and regulation, is surprising given the failure of one of the earliest, Long Term Capital Management (LTCM), that cost the banks dear. The fund, which launched in 1994, was famous because it had among its partners Nobel prize-winners Robert Merton and Myron S. Scholes. LTCM adopted the highly leveraged hedge fund formula of borrowing extensively and building chains of derivative betting 'on the margin', that is, based on a small outlay and sometimes no outlay. For its first few years, LTCM was hugely successful, building its partners a capital fund of $5 billion. The Fund initially raised total investments of $1.25 billion and arranged credit facilities with more than 50 banks. As Lowenstein records, LTCM exploited the banks' hunger for fees driving the most advantageous terms with the banks like 'hopeful parents' nurturing their 'incorrigible child' in the hope of future profits. He describes Merrill Lynch and Salomon Brothers as the main 'sugar daddies' in terms of financing

(Lowenstein 2001:82). According to Alan Greenspan, LTCM borrowed around $120 billion and had derivative positions worth around $1.25 trillion (Greenspan 2008:193–5). As Greenspan notes, it was hard to estimate overall leverage, but suggests it might have been 35:1. Elliott and Atkinson claim it might have been 100:1 (2008:264).

What brought down the fund was something the model was supposed to anticipate: the unexpected. In this case it was a default on debt by Russia. LTCM found itself with huge potential losses on its positions. As the biggest hedge fund, if it had had to unwind all its 'bets' the impact on the financial markets would have been enormous. It was deemed too big to fail and 16 of the world's biggest banks were called in by the Federal Reserve to put up rescue money of $3.6 billion to enable LTCM to unwind its positions slowly. The case was made to the banks that they would lose much more money if LTCM collapsed. Greenspan was also proud that no taxpayer's money was directly involved. It is clear from such a statement that the taxpayer is deemed to have no interest other than the tax implications of what banks do in their name. As Lowenstein puts it, LTCM was 'not an isolated instance but the latest in a series in which an agency of the government (or the IMF) has come to the rescue of private speculators' (2001:230). Despite the crash of LTCM and the earlier well-publicised example of the collapse of Barings in 1975, because of Nick Leeson's derivative trading, regulators seemed very sanguine.

Hedge funds are an emblem of the globalised casino economy, with most of their funds held offshore to avoid tax. They have had a huge impact on stock markets, currencies and other areas of financial speculation. Their very high levels of leverage also create great potential for financial volatility. As Janet Bush points out: 'If the hedge fund industry's positions in the market are twenty times the cash they hold, their potential impact on the world financial system is about equal to US GDP' (2006:27). At their peak, hedge funds had over $2 trillion invested and the BIS estimate of the size of the global derivative market was nearly $750 trillion. This compares with total global output of around

$60 trillion. Given their need for credit, hedge funds were early casualties of the credit crunch. Many were also caught up in the subprime market. By 2009 many funds in Europe and the US were either closed or running down their activities.

Credit-Driven Take-Overs: Private Equity

Private equity firms, like hedge funds, took advantage of the flood of cheap money to engage in speculative trading. However, their focus is not financial assets and derivatives, but trade in companies. Like hedge funds, most private equity firms are not listed on the stock exchange and fall outside the regulatory framework. They specialise in trading in existing companies, taking over private companies or taking stock market companies back into private ownership. Making money through mergers and acquisitions and asset stripping is not new and was condemned in the early 1970s by the British Prime Minister, Ted Heath, as the 'unacceptable face of capitalism'. Private equity firms claim that they are not asset strippers but make their money by streamlining a firm, making it more 'efficient' before selling it on at a profit. Private equity firms borrow extensively to buy companies, with a high ratio of borrowing to money directly invested. The borrowed money is usually placed on the balance sheet of the company purchased, rather than on the balance sheet of the private equity company. The aim of the private equity investor is to sell the company at a profit, despite the heavy debt the business carries. Private equity has proved to be very profitable with investors anticipating a 20 per cent return on their investment within three to six years and their activity has led to relatively small groups of people controlling company assets worth billions.

In February 2007 the British Prime Minister, Tony Blair, declared Britain to be one of the number one places in the world for private equity. Britain became a haven for private equity because it allowed tax relief on interest payments and also had a favourable tax rate for investment. Private equity is tax efficient in two ways. First, investment through debt is more tax efficient than equity finance. Second, a policy change in the UK in the late 1990s to encourage venture capital, that is, capital for new businesses, led to capital gains from investment being taxed at 10 per cent. Although they were not usually supporting new businesses, private equity companies benefited from this change. Also private equity partners were able to count their fee income as capital gain, thus paying 10 per cent tax and not 40 per cent as higher wage earners. One private equity director broke cover on this anomaly by pointing out that he paid less tax than his cleaning lady. Subsequently UK capital gains tax was raised to 18 per cent.

Leveraged private equity companies came to public notice through the takeover of the food and tobacco giant Nabisco in 1979 by the US firm KKR (Kohlberg, Kravis Roberts) (Burrough and Helyar 1990). This was followed by a steady stream of acquisitions by private equity companies in Britain and the US. At its height, one in five private sector workers in Britain, around 2.5 million people, were working directly or indirectly for a private equity company. This included many well-known names: Scottish and Newcastle, Canary Wharf, Anglia Water, Thames Water, Madame Tussauds, Kwikfit, Toys R Us, Little Chef, New Look, Odeon UCI, Travelodge, Matalan, United Biscuits, Associated British Ports, Pizza Express, Phones 4U, NCP, Twyford Bathrooms, Birds Eye and Gate Gourmet. The latter saw a bitter strike over pay and working conditions.

Several of the buyouts were controversial. When the British private equity firm Permira and its partners purchased the previously member-based Automobile Association in 2004, there was considerable disquiet. It was a very profitable purchase that made £300 million profit in three years. The purchase price was £1.75 billion, of which £1.3 billion was borrowed. Savings were made by cutting the 10,000 AA staff by one-third, and de-recognising the GMB trade union. Staff alleged that high pressure management tactics were being used and the morale of staff was at rock bottom. In 2003, a private equity consortium bought the UK department store Debenhams back into private ownership from the stock market. Two years later it was sold back to the stock market with the investors making more than three times their initial investment. Debenhams was left with debt of nearly £2 billion to face difficult trading conditions.

One of the last major private equity purchases before the crash was Alliance Boots, bought by a consortium led by KKR and an Italian entrepreneur. It was bought in 2007 for £11 billion of which £9.3 billion was debt. An investigative team from the *Guardian* newspaper reported that the cost of servicing this debt meant that Boots' debt costs rose from £25 million before the buyout to more than £600 million after. The *Guardian* team also maintain that much of this debt still lies on the lending banks' books, having fallen victim to the collapse of the securitisations market. Debt that had been traded was achieving only 60 per cent to 70 per cent of face value. There has also been a loss to the taxpayer. The consortium relocated Boots' headquarters to Switzerland and, as a result, £131 million of tax revenue has been lost (*Guardian* 9 February 2009). It is not only high street businesses that have been lumbered with huge debts by private equity speculation. Football clubs have also been prime targets. As a result of a buyout Manchester United is reported to have debts of around £700 million and Liverpool of around £350 million.

Robert Peston calculates that the major banks have lent up to $300 billion to fund private equity buyouts and much of this was securitised and sold on to the money markets (2008:176). He argues that the interest rates charged for these activities were too low given the level of risk. Also, loading the bought-out firms with huge debts to pay for management fees and high returns to investors could undermine the businesses by reducing their credit ratings. In March 2007, a report from the ratings agency Standard & Poor's indicated that private equity firms might be undermining the financial strength of Europe's corporate sector. The proportion of companies with debt rating as junk had risen from around 1 per cent in the early 1990s to 17 per cent in 2006. (Junk bonds offer high rates of return to take account of high levels of risk.) In the US the level might be as high as 50 per cent. Trades unions have also accused private equity companies of anti-Labour practices, excessive management fees, profiteering, asset stripping and dealing offshore to avoid corporation tax.

As private equity companies do not have to provide the same information as publicly quoted companies, back bench Labour MPs and trades unions called for more financial transparency, social and environmental reporting and the treatment of workers and suppliers to be monitored. In 2007 the British Private Equity and Venture Capital Association agreed a voluntary transparency code for around 200 private equity companies then operating in the UK.

In January 2009, a report on the private equity industry by Ernst and Young (published jointly with British Venture Capital Association), indicated that half the profits had come from using debt; around a third from the stock market rise and only a fifth from increased efficiencies (the main justification private equity companies give for their activities). Average return on investment was 330 per cent for the firms that had been sold on or floated with higher returns linked to higher debt. Levels of debt in ex-private equity companies was more than three times the level of debt in non-private equity companies. However, contrary to union criticisms, the report did not find marked evidence of job losses or asset stripping, but the very high level of debts made the firms involved very vulnerable in a credit crunch. The credit crunch also hit private equity badly as both credit and investment opportunities dried up. Many closed. The private equity firm 3i which is UK stock market quoted (and was itself a privatisation of a government agency) saw its share price fall by over 70 per cent during 2008.

Credit and Privatisation

A major impact of the shift from issue of money as notes and coin to the privatised issue of money as debt is that the state no longer has direct access to money issue. If the government cannot raise sufficient income from taxes, it has to borrow money from the private sector, mainly through issuing bonds. These are sold at a discount and repaid at face value. Having lost the ability to create its own money, the state has to get the private sector to create it for them by buying and trading in government bonds. Having to go to the private sector to raise funds limits the capacity for state expenditure, particularly when there is a philosophy that state borrowing 'crowds out' private investment. As Harvey points out, the state is put in a politically disadvantaged position if it has to borrow money from the private sector. He argues that from the 1980s onwards finance capital was able to move to centre stage, exercising power over state action. This, in turn, gave finance capital 'disciplinary power' over working class movements (Harvey 2003:64). New Labour helped this process by rejecting its roots in the Labour movement to court the new financial elite. One of its first acts was to revoke clause 4 of the Labour Party constitution that called for public ownership of the economy.

In Europe, a limitation on the state's access to the privatised money system was enshrined in the Maastricht treaty where government deficits, that is, higher public expenditure than government income, was not expected to go over 3 per cent of GDP. In Britain the solution was to borrow money through the private sector itself. Private companies would receive government contracts but initially finance the contracts themselves, receiving repayment over time. By setting up public-private partnerships, and particularly private finance initiatives (PFIs), state expenditure on capital projects could be moved off the state's balance sheet. PFIs were first introduced under John Major in 1992 and were greatly expanded when Labour came to power in 1997. By 2008 total investments had reached over £60 billion. Many PFIs were able to re-finance as interest rates fell and make additional profits, reportedly up to 100 per cent on the original contract. Such windfall profits were criticised by the National Audit Office. Critics have argued that PFI is an expensive way for governments to borrow money, as governments can raise money more cheaply than the private sector. Although the government benefits from taking the expenditure off its balance sheet in the short run, private finance adds to costs in the long run (Pollock 2004:26). Despite the claim that the private sector would bear any financial risk under private finance initiatives, in practice the government has had to meet the cost of projects in difficulties.

The government was forced to bail out the privatised London Tube contract and even more PFI contracts were in trouble as the economy contracted in 2008–09. PFI had proved to be a fair weather friend to the state.

A seeming solution to both the government's need to raise money and the demands of anti-state neo-liberal ideology was to sell government assets for cash. This led to a wave of privatisation of public utilities in Britain copied extensively in other parts of the world. Harvey has described privatisation as 'accumulation by dispossession', the conversion of collective state property to exclusive private property (2003:144–5). Like the private finance initiatives the state found itself having to rescue some of its privatisations, most notably renationalising Network Rail in 2001. The link between the ownership and control of finance and banking and the ability to accumulate through privatisation is most starkly exhibited in the demise of the Soviet Union and the fast track to capitalism that was imposed.

In *Sale of the Century* Freeland explores the way that privatisation of the financial system accompanied the acquisition of the formerly state-owned productive assets. In her study of one of the main oligarchs, Freeland points out that 'like so many of the future oligarchs, Potanin swiftly realised that the real money was to be made in banking' (2000:123). Valdimir Potanin formed his own bank by taking over the $300 million assets of one of the failing state banks. Through the bank he made loans to the new factory enterprises and held their accounts. Often these loans were exchanged for shares so that the bank eventually became the owner of the asset. Potanin also handled the state's customs agency account and the state arms trading agency. In the end he became the biggest Russian financial investment company, controlling 10 per cent of Russian GDP by 1997. She argues that this was a dangerous position to be in, as even Rockefeller at his most powerful only counted for 5 per cent of US GDP. As Freeland points out, most of the oligarchs made their money by getting hold of natural resource businesses or through banking, but mainly through handling large state accounts (2000:140).

The privatisation scramble was a combination of cheap money and cheap assets. Those who could get themselves into a position to bring the two together became the oligarchs. Freeland describes this as 'insider privatisation' with the consent of the government. Potanin followed the traditional banker's route to state assets by lending the government money in return for the right to manage state assets. When the government loans came up for payment the state assets were taken in lieu. Most of the oligarchs' banks failed, but they still held on to the assets acquired. As Freeland argues, 'the main thing was to create a capitalist system; it didn't really matter who the capitalists were' (2000:70). Freeland says, 'I couldn't help asking myself how different the Russian (oligarchs) really were from our own hero-entrepreneurs, the gizmo-makers and internet tycoons and financial wizards our society so fawningly lauds' (2000:180).

From Speculation to Fraud

One result of the lauding of financial wizards was the opportunity for fraud. The classic example was Charles Ponzi in the boom years before the 1929 crash. Ponzi schemes are those where there is no real investment and existing investors are paid out from the money from new investors. Such schemes can continue undetected as long as regulators don't look too closely and the investment market is growing. However, when new investment money dries up they are quickly exposed. The 2007–08 crash revealed a 15-year scam in the US by the aptly named Madoff, which might have netted $65 billion. When regulators looked at Madoff's books there was no evidence that he had ever traded a share on behalf of his investors, although he did file the required tax returns as if they had been made. The US Securities and Exchange Commission had received warnings as early as 1996 that Madoff's returns were too good to be true, but it didn't investigate, possibly because Madoff was a respected figure. Many rich people were defrauded in the Madoff scam, but so were banks and charities. The latter reflects the danger of trying to meet social need through the capitalist system. Rather than directly funnelling money to social needs, charities have to run the roller-coaster of bull and bear markets in order to create financial 'wealth'.

The neo-liberal ideology of the efficiency of markets, the demand for deregulation and the drive for speculative profits has created a climate that Black has described as 'criminogenic' with accounting as the 'weapon of choice' (2008). Practices include overstating asset values, lending to the worst borrowers to maximise income, covering up defaults, treating refinancing as new income, growing rapidly using Ponzi schemes and using off-balance-sheet to hide liabilities. Black argues that many people must know about these strategies including appraisers, internal accountants, officers and employees, rating agencies, computerised underwriters, stock analysts and external auditors. However as they are linked together in a 'responsibility tango' it is hard to identify where responsibility for losses and fraudulent behaviour lies. Black points out that only 200 of 35,000 Suspicious Activity Reports (SARs) submitted to the US Treasury led to prosecutions. He thinks the SARs represent only a fraction of the actual frauds and that it is almost impossible to prosecute in an environment of deregulation. He argues that the breakdown in interbank lending that led to the credit crunch could be because bankers do not trust other bankers, knowing the games that they play.

Examples of accounting frauds include Enron and Worldcom. Enron, which had engaged extensively in energy trading, misled investors on its viability telling its shareholders it had made profits of nearly $2 billion while telling the US tax service it had made a billion dollar loss. As well as criminal charges against senior Enron executives, three senior Merrill Lynch bankers were charged with aiding Enron by making a loan look like an asset by temporarily 'buying' three barges full of generators. Its auditors, Arthur Andersen, whose Houston office earned 25 per cent of its auditing revenue from Enron in addition to extensive consulting fees, collapsed shortly after. Worldcom's chief executive was jailed in 2005 for 25 years for an $11 billion fraud involving misleading financial information, including hiding $7 billion of operating expenses as capital expenditure (Glyn 2007:59). Other financial practices are more difficult to prove, such as insider trading or rumour mongering to manipulate the market. As Glyn points out, there is little incentive for transparency: underwriters seeking new business or aiming to not be caught with unmarketable shares have no incentive to warn customers or talk down share price (2007:60).

The Limits of Financialisation

> Speculators may do no harm as bubbles on a steady stream of enterprise. But the position is serious when enterprise becomes the bubble on a whirlpool of speculation. When the capital development of a country becomes a by-product of the activities of a casino, the job is likely to be ill-done.
>
> John Maynard Keynes 1936 (Stanford 2008:216)

Financialisation of the global economy has seemed to eclipse more traditional industries. Ingham has long argued that the two main aspects of capitalism, productive and financial, are inherently in conflict (1984). Capitalism is divided against itself. Finance seeks short term gain while productive capital needs long term investment. The financial sector is not just about the activities of a financial market (intermediation between those with capital and those who need capital), it is about the process of financial accumulation. In Ingham's terms financial capital (creditor capitalism) has triumphed over producer capitalism and it is this that has expanded on a global scale. With its financial resources, finance capital has its own power base. It is much more responsive and flexible than capital locked into factories or other concrete assets. The plethora of new financial instruments meant that 'the financial superstructure increasingly took on a life of its own' (Foster and Magdoff 2009:72). This was particularly true of the huge derivatives market that swamped world output many times over (Wigan 2009).

Foster and Magdoff see financialisation as the dominant force in neo-liberalism and globalisation. Productive capitalism is no longer creating opportunities for the accumulation of profit and attention has therefore turned to more rewarding places to invest and speculate. As the productive economy stalled, capital started to flow into the financial markets, not to invest in productive companies but to engage in trading and speculation in finance itself. Harvey agrees that lack of opportunities for profitable investment in productive capital drove the growth of finance capitalism (2003:88) while Brenner points out the period from 1973–93 was one of 'persistent stagnation' in the productive sector (2002:7). However, Foster and Magdoff do not agree with Ingham that financial capital has triumphed over producer capitalism. Instead they see a hybrid emerging that they call 'monopoly-finance capital' (2009:77).

Financial and productive companies are not on opposite sides in the contemporary financialised era. Rather they have both gone to the same side, non-financial and financial companies are both engaged in financial trading (Foster and Magdoff 2009:85). The most notable, of course, was Enron which started as a pipe laying company and ended up as speculators in energy trading. Foster and Magdoff build on Baran and Sweezy's classic analysis of Monopoly Capital (1966) to argue that the large productive monopolies of the twentieth century had surplus capital and nowhere to invest profitably. The innovations in the financial sector were an answer to their prayers. In the stage of monopoly finance capital: 'both production and finance under capitalism are at one and the same time both real and monetary in nature' (Foster and Magdoff 2009:70). However they see this seeming tangibility in the financial sector as illusory, in the end capitalism must return to its productive base. While countries may seem wealthy on paper, little can be shown for it. Paper asset value can be as ephemeral as the paper of which it is composed. Foster and Magdoff point to the great irony in the new era of financial investment: the stagnation and low profitability of the productive sector has been reproduced within the financial sector. In the financialised era, leverage is needed to enable profitable accumulation. Debt-based finance is driving the economy. However while elastic finance encourages capital to become flexible and mobile, it also leads to conditions of crisis.

Hence the need for Bio regional analysis.

Even at its most neo-liberal, the globalised financialised market system did not have it all its own way. Following the Asian financial crisis of 1997–98 Malaysia showed it was advantageous to re-impose capital controls (Abdelal 2007:185). In 1998 the Multilateral Agreement on Investment, which would have allowed global capital unfettered access to any domestic market, was defeated and, beginning in Seattle, from 1999 massive protests accompanied world trade talks. The Doha round of WTO talks finally collapsed in 2008 over the US's unwillingness to suspend its agricultural subsidies. Much of South America was politically diverging from neo-liberal globalisation. China was advancing steadily towards world leadership. By 2009 the Davos meeting of the neo-liberal capitalist and political elite was much more muted in the face of the changing political climate and economic collapse (Tett 2009:287). The anti-capitalist grass root movement continues to meet and organise to assert the existence of an alternative (Boaventura de Sousa 2006, Bennholdt-Thomsen et al. 2001).

Speculating with the People's Money

The argument put forward in this book is that although the money system is controlled by capitalist finance, it is still publicly underpinned by social trust and political authority. The money system is backed by the capacity of the state to borrow money on the basis of future taxation, or issue money that will be accepted as viable through the trust of the people. The money system therefore is only as strong as the solidarity of the society itself, and the capacity of the political authority to ensure payment of taxes or access other forms of national income. As the privatised issue of credit money through the banking system leads to speculation on a massive scale, it falls to the state authority to act as lender of last resort in a crisis. The unregulated money systems of the Anglo-American model of financialised capitalism have engaged in just such an orgy of credit creation for financial speculation. In doing so they are not using a private resource, or creating wealth, they are speculating with the people's money.

As has been argued in the chapter on banking, issuing bank credit money is equivalent to issuing 'fresh air' money in that there is no direct connection between the savings people deposit and the money banks lend out. Also as loans and savings cannot be distinguished from each other within the banking system, one person's loan becomes another person's savings. In the absence of state-issued fiat money, bank credit itself becomes the main source of money issue. Given the 'fresh air' nature of bank credit, this is also effectively fiat money. It is not issued on any substantive base: it is issued by the bank on the authority of the state. The benefit of fiat money is that it creates seigniorage for the issuer, that is, the benefit of the first use of that money over and above the cost of producing it. While state fiat money was the main basis of money issue, governments of all shades benefitted from its first use.

Seigniorage largely disappears when money is issued as debt. This is because money is no longer free at the point of issue. Not only must it be repaid, but repaid with interest. However, creating money as a borrower still enables control over the direction of the economy. Anyone who takes on bank-issued debt is making vital choices about priorities for the economy through how they choose to spend or invest that money. In a regulated banking system the organisations that create debt can be monitored and given rules on lending priorities. Under deregulation and innovative forms of lending, the impetus for credit creation has largely passed to the speculative financial sector. The widespread use of unregulated lending to act as high levels of leverage in speculative investment has created a new form of seigniorage. While borrowers have traditionally had to earn the money to repay their debts or invest in long term business projects, borrowing to leverage speculative deals is much more short term and potentially profitable. The benefit of the money issued to the borrower is much greater than the cost of its creation, that is, the interest paid on short term borrowing. Leverage with bank credit money means that borrowers can gain huge benefit for a small amount of personal investment. If the speculative gamble fails, it is the banking system, backed by the public sector, that has to pick up the pieces.

Despite the importance of the public sector to the security of the financial system, one notable aspect of the financialised super-rich is their reluctance to pay taxes. As Peston notes, they appear to have an aversion to making any contribution to the public sector (2008:16). The same is true of corporations with estimates of corporate tax avoidance in Britain of up to £13 billion. Failure to tax corporations and financial capital flows means that public and social infrastructure loses income, while there is more hot money washing around the global casino. William Brittain-Catlin (2006) sees financial developments from 1970 onwards as the disengagement of capitalism from nation states. This he describes as the off-shoring of capitalism through tax havens and off-shore finance. Multinational companies and banks have expanded globally to set up outlying 'vehicles' for these purposes. Most banks have off-shore operations or can arrange for clients to move their investments off-shore. The UK itself became an off-shore location for US financiers seeking to avoid both regulation and taxation. It was these off-shore activities that led to the push for more general deregulation, enabling the unrestricted movement of money across borders. As Richard Murphy points out, moving finance off-shore does not remove the liability of states. He notes that the Cayman Islands have financial commitments 500 times their income and Britain is unlikely to escape responsibility if there were to be a financial crisis there or in any other of the tax havens linked to the UK (2009:75).

While the failure to get rich individuals and financial companies to pay tax has a major impact on public expenditure, it also has implications for the financial system itself. There is the danger that the state will no longer be able to play its role of legitimating and underpinning finance. The same is true for the globalisation of money. What authority in the global domain will in the end guarantee payment? The modern banking system evolved through a close link between the needs of capitalism and the needs of the state. Financialised capitalism no longer wishes to keep its side of the bargain. While it will still supply the state with loans through the money market (if the state's credit rating is high enough), it is not willing to support the other important aspect of the money system, taxation. Since it is taxation that is the ultimate source of high powered money which underpins all other aspects of the money system, globalised money must be fragile.

The case that capitalism has made for private control of the money system is that it takes the risks that justify profits. Since it has become clear that it is society as a whole that carries the risk, there is no justification for the privileges of debt-fuelled privatised financialisation. Leveraged casino capitalism has linked the money creation system directly to speculative finance. This speculation feeds on itself so that financial asset prices become artificially inflated. When speculators base their leverage on bank credit they are reaping profits from the privatisation of what is, and what should be, a social and public resource. Not only do speculators exploit the socially grounded and publicly authorised banking system to feed speculative booms, the financially wealthy compound the problem by trying to avoid tax as far as possible. As it is the taxation base that ultimately underpins the banking system, this must end in crisis. In a democratic society it would be expected that the benefit of a public and social resource such as money would be to the benefit of society as a whole, not just to the few in a position to speculate.

Conclusion

The privatisation of the money system and the eclipsing (temporarily) of the role of the state, has meant that there had been little or no public control over money creation. This 'elastic' approach to money has fuelled financial speculation and accumulation. Through this process, capitalist individuals and companies have been able to project themselves as 'wealth creators' and the privatised banking system as the supporter of 'wealth creation'. 'Profitable' business has become the only basis upon which money can be legitimately issued and its interests must be prioritised at all times. Money issue for public or social reasons is deemed 'uneconomic' because it doesn't produce a profit. Yet the profit that capitalism claims can only be extracted through the continual issue of new money. Capitalism is issuing money to itself and claiming it as profit. While there may be some merit to capitalist claims if essential goods and services are being supplied along the way, when the activities of capitalist businesses are purely financial and speculative there can be no demonstrable benefit to the wider population of capitalist credit driven activities. Any claim of the capitalist system to be 'private' is dispelled if the money system it has harnessed rests on public and social support. While the benefits are private, the regime of accumulation rests on publicly grounded money. This has been clearly revealed during the financial crisis of 2007–08 which will be discussed in the next chapter.

5

THE FINANCIAL CRISIS OF 2007–08

The financial crisis of 2007–08 was not unheralded. As Paul Krugman argued in his book *The Return of Depression Economics*, first written in 1999 and re-issued in 2008, there were many earlier crises that were building up to what was likely to become another major depression. The 1990s alone saw crises in Latin America, East Asia, Japan and Russia. Argentina followed in 2001–02. Most notably, Japan had experienced a debt-fuelled property boom and collapse in the early 1990s from which it had not yet recovered. The 2007–08 crisis began in the US subprime housing market but quickly proved to have ramifications for banks in Europe and across the globe; states and regulating agencies struggled to find a response. From a subprime loan crisis it quickly became a banking and financial crisis and finally an economic crisis on a global scale. What was unexpected was the depth to which financial systems across the globe were undermined. What initially appeared to be a problem in the housing sector of one country in mid 2007 became a major crisis of the world financial system by October 2008 and a global economic recession/depression by 2009.

The Subprime Crisis

The subprime crisis was a trigger rather than a cause of the financial crisis. Mortgage finance was central to the financial innovations that had taken place in the banking sector. Mortgage backed securities were one of the main mechanisms by which banks began to tap directly into the money markets through the 'originate to distribute' sale of securitised debt. Following the collapse of the dotcom boom, money, particularly in the US, was very cheap but opportunities for profitable investment were limited. With US interest rates as low as 1 per cent, the returns on mortgage backed investments looked very good.

Mortgage lending was also an increasingly important source of income for the banks. Before the 1990s nearly two-thirds of British mortgages were issued through building societies. With the privatisation of building societies and the new mechanisms of raising loan finance, this had slumped to a fifth with high street banks taking the lion's share. In the US mortgages had traditionally been fixed interest and mainly underwritten by the large notionally private housing finance institutions, Fannie Mae (Federal National Mortgage Agency) and Freddie Mac (Federal Home Mortgage Corporation). Between them they provided backing for half the nation's mortgages worth around $5 trillion.

What changed in the US was the introduction of adjustable rate mortgages. By 2007 nearly 50 per cent of US mortgages were issued as variable rate. Mortgage finance had become financially exciting with its huge new sources of income through the securitisation of loans and a new market for home loans in the subprime and equity release markets. With house prices rising, many people were sitting on homes worth much more than their current mortgage commitments. They could be readily encouraged to 'release' that value, that is, take on more debt, or hand over rights to their home in return for cash. New mortgage companies were sprouting up knowing that there was a ready secondary market for any mortgages they could persuade people to take. Low income house owners were particularly welcome as they could be charged a higher level of interest. It seemed a win-win situation. People could now afford houses, or raise money from their existing house. Mortgage companies could take their fee and sell on their loans. Banks could take their fee and sell on the securitised mortgage to investors who were hungry for higher returns. Of course there were risks, but these were being dealt with by risk assessment mechanisms, insurances and, in the last resort, the collateral of house value. Risk assessment for traditional mortgage lending was through careful scrutiny of the borrower. The new way of assessing creditworthiness was not carried out at the level of the individual mortgage borrower, but through statistical calculations and profiling. Measures were used such as age, location or type of property. The security for the lenders was through another innovation, Credit Default Swaps (CDS). For a fee, banks and institutions would guarantee the securitised loans against default. The swaps tended to be private unregulated 'over-the-counter' arrangements between financial institutions.

There were massive flaws in this system. House-buyers were able to raise loans easily even with low incomes. Information given when taking out a mortgage, including ability to pay, was not verified. This led to the notorious NINJA loans: no income no job no questions asked. The reason for such a casual approach was that those issuing the mortgage intended to sell on the debt very quickly. This meant there was little incentive to minimise risk by more careful scrutiny. Also, very dubious methods were used to pressure people into taking out mortgages, mainly in the form of deals that seemed very good but only lasted for a short time. For US house owners used to a fixed rate mortgage, it was natural to assume that the original rate of payment would continue. These problems were ignored because any risk would be swiftly passed on from house buyers who might have problems paying, through mortgage issuers who would sell on the loan, to investors who would be covered by an insurance against default. The claim was that everyone benefitted as the risk was spread widely. However as it turned out, spreading risk widely did not mean that risk could be avoided, rather it spread to all lenders and investors, contaminating the whole lending process (Brummer 2008:42).

The problems in the subprime market emerged as the boom in US house prices started to slow from 2004 onwards. When prices started to turn downwards in 2006, it became clear that the subprime mortgage market was particularly shaky. Defaults on mortgages within the first three months were virtually unheard of but they were starting to happen. The main reason for this was the dramatic increase in the sale of mortgages to poorer families. As national mortgage agency executives later admitted, they knew about problems relating to subprime loans from 2004 but were under pressure from the US government to provide more homes for low income families. As defaults began to grow, the problem could no longer be ignored and hundreds of mortgage companies started to go out of business (Phillips 2008:8–9).

As mortgages started to default, the primary fallback position for the lender also disappeared: the value of the houses themselves. A core assumption of the house price boom was that house prices had conquered gravity and wouldn't fall. Even this may not have triggered a general crisis in the financial system, if it were not for the way the mortgage securities had been packaged and sold. The innovative way of raising money through securitising and selling loans had seemed to offer almost unlimited sources of funding for the banks and profitable investment for investors. What undermined the system was the process of 'slicing and dicing' the packages of mortgages. Mortgage backed securities had been bundled into collatoralised debt obligations (CDOs) and sold to a range of investors at different levels of interest and priority for payment in the event of default. As these investments were guaranteed against non-payment through the swap mechanism they seemed to be secure. Also as the mortgage market was generally seen as a safe area for investment, MBSs were given the triple A status by the rating agencies that institutional investors needed. Since World War II, mortgage lending, particularly in the US, had been very stable with no history of major defaults. This, together with a rising housing market, made even subprime mortgages look like good investments. While this might have been true in the early stages of the securitisation revolution, the viability of many of the later MBSs issued was very doubtful, given the associated problems of poor risk assessment and high pressure sale of dubious mortgages.

Rising defaults and falling house prices began to cast doubt upon the whole mechanism of securitisation. For institutional investors at least, the investment was supposed to be safe, but the value even of their first tranche securities collapsed, because no-one knew who held the defaulting mortgages. Rather than spreading risk through mortgage-based securities, it seemed as if investors were going to have to share incalculable risk because any of the 'structured investment' packages could be contaminated by risky debt. In 2008 up to $900 billion could be locked into such CDOs (Blackburn 2008:96). Throughout 2007 and 2008 the losses in the subprime sector spread to the wider housing market in both the US and the UK. In the US, commentators such as Professor Nouriel Roubini predicted an overall fall in house prices of 40–45 per cent. By early 2009 UK house prices had fallen by around a sixth and housing sales were down by 70 per cent. Despite interest rates plunging to almost zero the housing market was effectively dead in both the US and the UK.

The subprime crisis became a crisis for the banks when they could no longer sell on their securitised packages or price their credit-related assets. There was a two-fold problem. First, they had made loans that would now have to sit on their balance sheets because they could not sell them. Second, many of those loans could be defaulting. The whole securitised system had been a merry-go-round of buying and selling debts and risks. Regulated and non-bank financial institutions were, at the same time, buyers and sellers of securities and guarantors of risk. Through mechanisms such as credit default swaps there had been an attempt to spread risk, but this made it even harder to see where the actual risk among the 'counter-parties' lay. The problem was that what looked like a well-balanced hedge system was really everyone taking in everyone else's washing and using the same soap packet. As the price of assets could not be gauged, investors in the money markets such as sovereign wealth funds, hedge funds, pension funds or companies seeking to make money on their cash flows fled the market. Equally the interbank lending market, which should have been the most established and safest, closed down. The London Interbank Offered Rate (LIBOR) is the basis upon which banks lend to each other in the short term. When this stopped functioning in August 2007 it signalled that even the most established institutions did not trust each other. In particular, they would not accept credit-based securities as collateral for loans. As the optimism and trust that had underpinned the whole securitised and financialised system melted away, the whole edifice of collateralised finance collapsed, resulting in what was quickly labelled the credit crunch (Brummer 2008, Mason 2009, Morris

2008, Pym and Kochan 2008, Turner 2008, Tett 2009). Lending institutions, saddled with unknown levels of risk, refused to offer any more credit in any direction.

Northern Rock

One very visible sign of the credit crunch was the run on Northern Rock bank in the UK (Brummer 2008, Walters 2008). This was the first run on a UK bank since 1866. Northern Rock, a demutualised former building society, had been seen as a leader in the UK mortgage field, particularly for first time buyers. In the first six months of 2007 it had increased its share of the mortgage market by over 50 per cent and was issuing one in five of all UK mortgages. It was also helping to spread home ownership by offering not only 100 per cent mortgages, but 125 per cent 'Together' mortgages that formed a quarter of its loan book. Northern Rock was also one of the lenders most engaged in raising funds through securitisation, making it one of the most highly leveraged banks in Europe. It had adopted this model because it did not have an extensive branch network to attract savings. Unlike building societies such as the Nationwide with 700 branches that could balance 75 per cent of its loans by savings, Northern Rock could only cover around a quarter (£24 billion savings as against loans of around £100 billion). Adam Applegarth, the Chief Executive of Northern Rock, had been lauded for enthusiastically embracing the new way of raising funds. To aid the securitisation process, Northern Rock had set up Granite, a special purpose investment vehicle, as a separate trust based in the Channel Islands. Granite sold bundles of mortgages, nearly 30 per cent of which were 'Together' loans. This model worked well until the market for these securities began to dry up in the summer of 2007 as the subprime crisis started to bite.

The trigger for the run on Northern Rock on 14 September 2007 was a media report that it had needed to go to the Bank of England to borrow extra funds because it could not raise money from other banks. The run began on a Friday and although the government and Bank of England issued generalised assurances over the weekend, the run continued with Northern Rock paying out around a billion pounds a day. The possibility of the collapse of Northern Rock meant that around 6,000 employees were faced with the loss of their jobs, thousands of savers with the loss of their savings above the banking system's compensation scheme guarantee level of £35,000 (subsequently raised to £50,000) and shareholders with a collapse of their shares, many of whom were original members of the Northern Rock Building Society. Northern Rock was also an important organisation for the north east of England where it was based. As well as providing local employment, 5 per cent of Northern Rock's pre-tax profits were put into a foundation that funded a wide range of social, sporting and cultural activities in the region.

By Monday 17 September, facing continued queues outside the bank and rumbles about the viability of other banks and building societies, the treasury guaranteed all deposits currently in place. Although the bank regulators had issued reassurances over the weekend, savers were only satisfied when a clear statement of support was made by the Chancellor, Alastair Darling, himself. The run could only be stopped when the government gave its full backing to all Northern Rock savers, and thereby implicitly (although certainly not at that time explicitly) to all savers throughout the banking system. Mervyn King, the Governor of the Bank of England, was initially reluctant to bail out the bank. In a letter to the Parliamentary Treasury Select Committee on Wednesday 12 September 2007 he argued the principle that to provide funds to supplement the ailing financial market would encourage 'moral hazard', that is, it would encourage even more risky behaviour in the future. He also argued against cutting interest rates as this 'penalizes those financial institutions that sat out the dance, encourages herd behaviour and increases the intensity of future crises'. A week later his hand was forced and resources were made available, £10 billion to the whole banking sector, of which Northern Rock borrowed £8 billion. This was only the beginning of what would eventually become a flood of financial support to the banking sector.

In the next few months, with the Directors and Chief Executive of Northern Rock resigning, or being pushed, the government started a search for private bidders to no avail. In February 2008 Northern Rock was nationalised. By this time it was worth £380 million compared with its peak value of £5 billion. Share prices which had peaked at £12 were worth only 90p. There was great concern that a nationalised bank would have a competitive advantage and over the next few months Northern Rock was careful not to undercut other banks and building societies. Even so, by September 2008 it had repaid half of its government loans. However by 2009 as the crisis worsened, far from running down its business the state-run Northern Rock was being asked by the government to increase its lending to support desperate home owners and businesses.

Although the financial innovations on which the Northern Rock business model, and that of many other banks, had been based had severe weaknesses, the new method of raising bank funds was not questioned by the UK Financial Services Agency which was responsible for regulating and monitoring bank activity. For failing to spot the flaws in the new practices, the UK Treasury Select Committee declared the Financial Services Authority guilty of a 'systematic failure of duty'. The tripartite regulatory system that Gordon Brown as Chancellor had set up was also widely questioned. However the UK regulatory failure was shared with regulatory authorities in Europe and America. Lord Turner, Chair of the FSA, later admitted that his organisation had missed systemic risk because they were concentrating on individual organisations, rather than getting the wider picture. People had tried to raise the alarm. One former risk manager with HBoS (Halifax Bank of Scotland) claimed he had been sacked for warning of undue risk. The following furore led to the ex-head of HBoS, Sir James Crosby, resigning as Deputy Chair of the FSA.

What was clear was that states could not stand by and watch their banks fail. The legislation that went through the British parliament to nationalise Northern Rock was not specific and could allow the government to nationalise other banks if necessary. As bank lending collapsed, the US Federal Reserve

Board and the European Central Banks made substantial loans to their banking sectors, around $300 billion in the first instance, to increase liquidity. This was to be the beginning of many attempts by governments and central banks to replenish the money available to the banks and encourage them to start lending again. Over the next 18 months a range of measures were implemented. These included loans to create liquidity, funds for the purchase of problematic securities, insurance for new and old debt, funds for recapitalisation and nationalisation. Like the UK, the US increased deposit insurance, from $100,000 to $250,000.

As the months went by it was clear that despite huge sums of money and insurances being made available to them in various ways, the banks were unwilling to commit themselves to any further lending. In Britain mortgages were only available to purchasers with large deposits and at high rates compared with the rock bottom base rate. The low base rate was actually reducing money supply as many people with 'tracker' mortgages that tracked national interest rates were eagerly paying off their loans, £8 billion was repaid in the last quarter of 2008 alone. Between August 2007 and August 2008 central banks pumped upwards of $650 billion liquidity into their banking systems. The problem with bad debts and uncertainty about 'toxic' assets was compounded by a collapse in the value of bank shares. January 2008 saw the biggest global stock markets fall since 9/11 with banks as big losers.

As 2008 progressed it became clear that pumping liquidity into the banks wasn't working and that capital values were getting dangerously low threatening solvency.

Financial Crisis

While the run on Northern Rock was spectacular evidence of the crisis, investment banks were already well aware of the oncoming problems. By early 2007 doubts were being raised about the value of the securitised packages and by the summer funds that had been heavily investing in them started to fail. Bear Stearns, a large US investment bank with substantial exposure to MBSs, saw two funds fail and many Wall Street banks faced substantial losses. In Europe three German banks were facing mortgage-based losses and the French bank BNP Paribas had to suspend three investment funds (Brummer 2008:57–60). Bear Stearns alone had total exposure to bad debts of over $200 billion (Mason 2009:8). By March 2008 it was clear that Bear Stearns could not recover from its problems and its shares that once traded at $170 were near to worthless. As technically the Federal Reserve could not bail out an investment bank, JP Morgan Chase was given $30 billion to buy it. This was an important turning point in the crisis as the Federal Reserve, by supporting an investment bank, had stepped beyond the regulated banking system and was directly supporting the financial markets.

In July 2008 the US had faced a further crisis when the national mortgage agencies Fannie Mae and Freddie Mac lost more than half their value on the stock market and faced losses of $14 billion as mortgage defaults rose. By the end of 2008 Freddie Mac shares had fallen 77 per cent. The then US Treasury Secretary Henry (Hank) Paulson moved quickly to pledge unlimited government backing including the purchase of equity, which Paulson described as 'conservatorship' rather than nationalisation. This acknowledged what many commentators had argued: that the private status of these organisations was a 'necessary fiction' as they could never be allowed to fail (Brummer 2008:19–20). Fannie Mae, originally a government agency, had been privatised by Lyndon Johnson in 1968 so that the government books would look better given the high cost of the Vietnam War.

September 2008 was another critical turning point when the more than 150-year-old US investment bank Lehman Brothers, with 25,000 employees, was allowed to fail. Lehman had been heavily involved in the credit derivative market and in 2007 was leveraged at $29 to each dollar invested (Tett 2009:172). Tett illustrates the escalation of crises in the financial sector. In 1978 when LTCM had failed it could be rescued for under $4 billion. The hole in Lehman's books could be anywhere from $30 to $60 billion (Tett 2009:272). The collapse also brought down long-established money market funds. Soros sees the collapse of Lehman as very significant. Investment funds are supposed not to lose their original capital invested, but one of the oldest and most established funds 'broke the buck' (2008:312).

Letting Lehman fail was an attempt to let the market take its course. According to neo-classical economic theory the market is a self-correcting mechanism that will heal itself. Far from a self-correcting response, there was a massive loss of confidence in the banking system generally, so much so that, as Mason argues, it came close to 'meltdown' (2009:1–7). The Lehman failure sent the financial system into a tail-spin. None of the investment banks survived the crisis, with Goldman Sachs and Morgan Stanley applying to change their status from investment banks to bank holding companies and thereby come under state regulation and support. Merrill Lynch, which had sold a total of $52 billion CDOs in 2006, topping the league, (Tett 2009:158) was taken over by Bank of America with government support. However, by January 2009 Bank of America was itself looking for government loans. The corporations that had dabbled in finance to great profit also found themselves in difficulties. In December 2008 the General Motors Acceptance Company, General Motor's finance arm, facing losses of $8 billion, registered as a bank holding company to access government funding. The state was having to support all sectors of the financial system from regulated banks, to investment banks, to finance companies.

Only days after letting Lehman fail, the US Treasury was forced to take 80 per cent ownership of one of the world's biggest credit insurers, AIG (American International Group), investing up to $175 billion by April 2009. AIG had assets of $1 trillion but at least a third of this was insurance on worthless debt (Mason 2009:13). Loan insurance was one of the largest credit derivative markets. The International Swaps and Derivatives Association estimated the total credit default market in 2008 was worth $55 trillion, roughly equivalent to world output. As the market was unregulated there were anomalies such as there being many more CDSs than the bonds and trades they insured. Creating CDSs provided a good income for financial institutions as long as the risk of failure was low. What the market now faced was major defaults and the possibility of paying several insurances on each loan. Hedge funds, as ever the carrion crows of finance, were busily buying up CDSs cheaply in the hope that they could make a full cost claim as loans failed.

Problems in the credit insurance market threatened a major aspect of US public sector finance, 'monoline' insurance. Monoline insurers guaranteed billions of dollars of local and municipal bonds, a very common form of public funding in the US. When these organisations strayed into insuring mortgage backed securities, their viability was threatened. The traditional monoline market was very safe with many institutional investors. If defaulting loans meant that monocline credit ratings were downgraded institutional investors would have to withdraw. A crisis in the monolines would therefore make it very difficult for US local authorities to raise funds through issuing bonds. Central to the credit insurance market was the reliability of the credit rating agencies. Institutional investors, in particular, required investments to have the key Triple A rating. As the crisis evolved, the independence of the rating agencies was being questioned as they were paid by the issuers of credit-based securities to carry out the ratings. As part of the fall out, Standard and Poor's and Moody's were called before the US Senate's Securities and Exchange Commission to answer accusations of a conflict of interests and that they had been asleep at the wheel.

As the crisis escalated, estimates of total potential losses grew. In July 2008 the IMF Global Financial Stability Report thought they could reach $1trillion. Morris changed the title of his book between printings from *The Trillion Dollar Meltdown* to *The Two Trillion Dollar Meltdown* (2008). By 2009 Gillian Tett was reporting estimates of total losses of up to four trillion dollars (2009:ix). The failure of Lehman Brothers had been catastrophic for the banks because it led to a major collapse in banking shares, threatening insolvency (Langley 2010). Another collapse in bank shares followed in January 2009, reflecting a series of very poor bank results for 2008. By the end of January 2009 many banks in Britain and the US had lost up to 90 per cent of their value, including Citigroup in the US and Bradford and Bingley, Royal Bank of Scotland (RBS) and Halifax Bank of Scotland (HBoS) in the UK. Citigroup, which was worth $250 billion in 2007, saw its value collapse to $21 billion in 2008 (Mason 2009:51). Much of this volatility was blamed on hedge funds 'shorting' bank shares, that is, selling shares they do not own in the hope of buying them more cheaply later. The US and UK governments were so concerned about bank shares being shorted during the crisis that for a time they banned all short trade. Later it was resumed, but speculators buying a substantial number of shares had to declare what they were doing.

The combination of collapsing capital values and assets in the form of outstanding loans turning toxic meant that banks no longer had sufficient secure assets to match their liabilities. Banks tried to rebalance their businesses by getting rid of their bad debts and raising more capital and deposits. According to an IMF Global Financial Stability Report, banks had written off $400 billion of bad debts by July 2008. Throughout 2008 banks continued to write off, or write down, their assets: UBS and Citigroup wrote down $19 billion each and Merrill Lynch $17 billion (Mason 2009:104). Nouriel Roubini has calculated that global bank write-offs could reach $2 trillion out of $10 trillion toxic assets (in Mason 2009:106).

To try to rescue their dire financial position several banks launched rights issues or raised new loans. This worked for a short time in the early stages of the crisis. In Britain the Royal Bank of Scotland successfully raised new equity of £12 billion despite what was later revealed to be its dire financial position. A request for £4 billion by HBoS failed badly and Bradford and Bingley had to withdraw a rights issue following a near 50 per cent drop in share price. Barclays successfully raised more than £11 billion from sovereign wealth funds and private investors in the Middle East and Asia. Even so, Barclays lost 70 per cent of its share value between October 2008 and January 2009. US banks also looked for support from sovereign wealth funds. Sovereign wealth funds are cash funds held in major reserve currencies in oil-exporting or export trading countries. Although they belong to the national government, they are invested as commercial funds. Holders of large funds are China, Singapore and the Middle East. The total held in sovereign wealth funds in 2007 was around $3 trillion (Tett 2009:245) and it is expected to rise considerably in future years. Several banks received injections of capital from these sources including Merrill Lynch, Citigroup, UBS and Morgan Stanley. The intervention of sovereign wealth funds muddies the waters between public and private involvement in the banking system. It raises a question as to whether countries will be held liable for the activities of their banking system if sovereign wealth funds lose substantial amounts of money in the banking debacle (Gowan 2009:28).

The Public to the Rescue: Saving the Banks

As bank shares collapsed and the toxic debt problem showed no sign of abating, state support started to shift towards partial or total nationalisation. In Britain, September 2008 saw the collapse and nationalisation of the demutualised building society Bradford and Bingley, which had been very exposed to the buy-to-let market. Its savings arm was bought by the Spanish bank Santander which had earlier bought two other former building societies, Alliance and Leicester and Abbey National. Santander had largely escaped the subprime crisis because of tough Spanish regulations on off balance sheet activities. The British government also took majority ownership of the Royal Bank of Scotland (RBS) for £20 billion, invested £17 billion in Halifax Bank of Scotland (HBoS) and arranged for the latter to be bought by Lloyds TSB. Despite the fact that the new £30 billion bank would be 43 per cent owned by the government with nearly 28 per cent of UK mortgages and one-third of its current accounts, few of the concerns about unfair competition raised at the time of the Northern Rock nationalisation were made. By the time the formal changeover took place in January 2009, a further collapse in shares meant the combined company was only worth £10 billion equivalent to HBoS's £10 billion losses in 2008.

State support for banks was also taking place in the US, with the government taking a large stake in Citigroup and injecting capital to support several other banks. At times the US and UK governments were putting in more capital than the banks were worth. The Swiss Banking giant UBS faced huge losses and needed state support, as did Fortis in the Benelux countries. The staid Rhineland German banks did not escape. The German government had to make substantial provisions for toxic debt and took stakes in its second largest bank, Commerzbank, and the big mortgage lender Hypo Real Estate. Even Deutsche Bank made a loss of nearly €4 billion in 2008, its first loss in 50 years. Being a state run bank did not help. The state owned regional bank, Bayern Landesbanken, suffered substantial losses. Nor did building societies escape: in Britain several had to be taken over or merged including the Derbyshire, Cheshire and the Dunfermline in Scotland, which collapsed due to exposure to commercial loans.

The problems for the banks became even clearer when they posted their 2008 results early in 2009. In Britain, the bailed out bank RBS had made a loss of more than £24 billion, the biggest in British corporate history. Most of this loss resulted from involvement in a disastrous £47 billion takeover of the Dutch bank ABN Amro at the top of the market in October 2007. This deal went ahead even after Northern Rock had collapsed. The market response to this result was a share price collapse to 11p at one point, making the company worth around £4.5 billion, requiring further government support, taking its stake to nearly 70 per cent. Once the scale of the loss became known, there was public revulsion at the fact that the boss of RBS at the time of the crisis had voluntarily left the bank with a full pension of over £700,000 a year. Under intense pressure he later offered to give up part of the pension. The fact that such a huge payment was not questioned at the time is a sign of the cosy relationship between civil servants, government and senior financial executives. It seemed as if financial executives had a divine right to receive lavish financial rewards, win or lose. Widespread public anger was not helped by the RBS putting £325 billion into the government's toxic debt insurance scheme. As the bank could not pay the premium for this insurance, or the 10 per cent it would have to pay towards any debts written off, it looked as if the government stake in the business might need to go up to 80 or 90 per cent. Another part nationalised bank, Lloyds/HBoS, indicated £260 billion of troubled assets might need to go into the government debt insurance scheme.

By January 2009 total bank bailouts and potential costs in the UK were at least £600 billion, more than 100 per cent of the UK budget before the crisis began. Projected actual expenditure could be up to £200 billion according to the IMF (Tett 2009:288). Total bank liabilities resting with the public could total £3 trillion, more than twice GDP, with more pessimistic estimates going up to £5 trillion. It has been estimated by New York Professor Nouriel Roubini that losses in the US financial system could reach $3.6 trillion before the crisis ends. Banks swallowed up the billions of dollars, pounds and euros and yet the credit crunch still continued. Despite large inputs of public money, banks were reluctant to lend because of the level of toxic debt they carried. Governments tried to help this process by buying up or insuring this debt. The UK government insurance scheme offered to guarantee 90 per cent of all bad debts, with banks meeting the first 10 per cent of failures. The aim was to make banks feel more secure about this debt and therefore more willing to lend again to desperate businesses and households. The danger was that banks, far from being more willing to lend to new borrowers or support their existing borrowers, would use the facility to close down accounts, thus putting firms relying on regular bank credit out of business.

Sir James Crosby, former head of HBoS, commissioned by the British government to report on the housing crisis, saw no end to the liquidity crisis. One-third of the bonds relating to the securitised products that had been issued were up for renewal by 2010 and there was no likelihood of ready funds forthcoming. The credit creation gap was huge. For example, the UK bank HBoS had been borrowing £1.78 for every £1 deposited (Mason 2009:15). Northern Rock had borrowed £3 to every £1. Highly leveraged investment banks and hedge funds were looking at ratios of 30:1 and higher. Government action through the banking system had failed to work because the activities of the banks could not be separated from the rest of the financial sector, particularly the shadow banking system linked to the money markets. Non-banks were issuing credit and regulated banks were engaged in speculative trading. The BBC's Robert Peston has estimated that governments around the world have committed around $14.5 trillion to support the world's banks and Mason agrees that a 'conservative estimate' could be up to $15 trillion, with $8.5 trillion of that in the US and €2.7 trillion in Europe (Mason 2009:53).

Despite the large amounts of liquidity and recapitalisation and, in many cases, reasonably healthy reserves, banks were still not willing to lend. The credit mechanisms of privatised finance were no longer working. Profitability within the financial sector had been enhanced by leverage. Borrowed money had boosted returns on the much smaller amount of invested capital. The search for returns had sought out more and more risky financial assets. Like any speculative pyramid it depends on continued liquidity. As Chuck Prince, then Chair and CEO of Citigroup, once famously put it, 'When the music stops in terms of liquidity, things will be complicated. But as long as the music is playing, you've got to get up and dance. We're still dancing.' (Langley 2010).

Economic Crisis

By the end of 2008 it was clear that the catastrophic activities of speculative financial dancers was finally impacting on the productive economy, which had seemed for a time to be able to ride out the storm. The productive and trading sectors had begun to run out of money. The UK faced a wave of company collapses in November 2008 including Woolworths, MFI, Adams, Findus and JRB. The US formally went into recession at the end of 2008 and in early 2009 saw a drop in the US price index for the first time in 50 years. The automobile industry was in crisis and despite substantial government support General Motors filed for bankruptcy in June 2009. Unemployment around the world rose sharply and the OECD was predicting a sharp fall in world trade. Given the way that debt had fuelled economic growth, global economies now faced the danger of debt deflation that Irving Fisher identified in 1933. Outstanding debt would demand that assets be sold, driving prices down and so making the debt even higher in relation to remaining assets. From a peak of $63 trillion in 2007 world stock markets lost half their value in the crash (Mason 2009:53).

The huge floods of money in the financial markets had led to the commitments of the financial sector being much bigger than the GDP in many countries. If the 'Chartalist' theory of money is correct and money is only a token that rests on the ultimate viability of the taxation basis of the economy in which it sits, then most national economies were bankrupt. The Royal Bank of Scotland with its £1.8 trillion balance sheet could outstrip UK GDP and the total of UK banks' balance sheets could top nearly £5 trillion. The first country to be affected systemically by the crisis was Iceland, which had for some time been considered a small jewel of prosperity. With a population of around 300,000, Icelandic banks had gone on a major international borrowing and investment spree offering very good interest rates to attract inward investment. As the banking crisis escalated, it became clear that the banking system had liabilities that were around ten times the GDP of the country.

In October 2008 Landsbanki, parent of the online bank Icesave, a hitherto 'best buy' investment which had attracted many British people, local authorities, organisations and charities, was nationalised and put into receivership. This was followed by the other two main banks Kaupthing and Glitnir. The impact on the national economy was evidenced in the collapse of the krona. Interest rates rose to nearly 30 per cent and Iceland was forced to go to the IMF for an emergency loan. The perils of the free flow of money and international financial systems were clear when the UK government had to lend Iceland the money to reimburse UK savers in Icelandic banks in order to maintain confidence in its own banking system. Because Iceland had always had high interest rates many Icelandic people had borrowed to buy houses and cars in other currencies, often encouraged by Icelandic banks themselves. Now those loans had almost doubled in value. Similar problems were experienced in Eastern European countries such as Hungary, where reputedly up to 90 per cent of mortgages were in external currencies (mainly Swiss francs and Japanese yen).

Ireland was another economic star that fell to Earth. By early 2009 the banking system was in crisis and the government was forced to guarantee all of its banks' deposits, a commitment worth double its GDP. Countries in trouble were facing having their government's credit status downgraded with ramifications for the cost of raising loans and debt insurance. Even Britain was facing a possible write-down in its credit rating and the impact of the crisis on the British national economy was clear. At the end of 2008 the pound tumbled by 25 per cent against the euro and fell back very sharply against the dollar, from a high of around $2 to $1.4.

During late 2008, and certainly by the beginning of 2009, it was clear that putting money or capital into the banks was not enough. Money was needed in the economy as a whole. Governments around the world dropped all pretensions of the independence of markets and started to pump money into their financial sectors and the wider economy. This was done through a combination of fiscal stimulus (government tax and expenditure) and the obscurely named 'quantitative easing'. This is a euphemism for the government reclaiming the role of money creation. In March 2009 Ben Bernanke, head of the Federal Reserve, announced what he called a 'credit easing' of $1 trillion by buying $300 billion of US Treasury bonds and $700 billion of mortgage securities from Freddie Mac and Fannie Mae. By 2009 the UK had made £200 billion available through quantitative easing. On election, Barack Obama had announced a stimulus package worth $800 billion. This was on top of Paulson's $700 billion TARP (Troubled Assets Relief Programme) and Treasury Secretary Tom Geithner's proposed $1 trillion financial rescue package. As a result of the crisis, the UK and US budgets had doubled. Interest rates dropped to 0.5 per cent in the UK and 0.25 per cent in the US, the lowest in history.

Quantitative easing can operate in a number of ways. Government can buy corporate bonds from the markets to help businesses get ready cash. The government can also buy its own debt back, again giving cash to the holder. The central bank can also release money to the treasury by purchasing long term treasury bills, that is, providing the government directly with money. This is direct money creation, a measure used by Roosevelt in the Great Depression. The fact that the announcement of the quantitative easing proposals produced a bounce in the stock market shows that capitalism has no problems with printing money when it can benefit. The danger in quantitative easing through the financial sector (the UK approach) is that the money will just go to the same people who have contributed to the financial collapse. Direct lending to productive companies or supporting mortgage debt at the level of the household could produce much more immediate results. There are many constructive ways in which new money can be issued and these will be discussed in the final chapter.

Despite all the efforts by states to restart their economies and their financial systems, success is not inevitable. Japan has tried a range of measures since its crash in the early 1990s. It has had interest rates near 0 per cent since 2001. This only fed a 'carry' trade where speculators borrowed in yen to invest in countries with higher interest rates. Recapitalisation of banks with trillions of yen to cover bad debts has not worked. Fiscal stimulus has led to public debt of 150 per cent of GDP and quantitative easing has been tried without notable positive success since 2001–02. Japan has tried cash payments to all households, loans for people between jobs, tax cuts for home-owners, support for banks and credits for small business, all to little avail. This may be a combination of the overhang of debt and property asset deflation Japan experienced and the fact that its economy is still export dependent. Mason argues that the measures tried in Japan, while not bringing positive results, may have stopped things from being worse (Mason 2009:47). Japan also shows that a country can survive without a constant growth dynamic and its degree of inequality is much less than the Anglo–American economies. It may, however, be evidence that a market-oriented economy is no longer a viable way forward for late industrial economies.

In April 2009 a G20 Summit was held in London to try to get a co-ordinated response to the global financial crisis. It offered no fundamental reforms of the banking system or the financial sector, but it did establish the basis for international co-operation and regulation. It proposed to upgrade the Financial Stability Forum established in 1999 by the Bank of International Settlements to become a Financial Stability Board to monitor risk and provide early warning reporting to the G20, the IMF and central bank governors. Financial institutions, instruments and markets were to be subject to tighter regulation and accountability standards. Pay and bonuses should reflect risk. All banks would need to increase their reserves, including foreign currency, and be counter-cyclical, that is increase reserves in good times with possible borrowing restrictions in boom conditions. Hedge funds and private equity companies should be regulated and be more transparent about leverage, strategy and risk. Credit derivatives should be traded formally with tighter rules for credit rating agencies. There would be an end to secrecy in tax havens. It remains to be seen if governments have the political will or power to impose these reforms. The IMF was a major winner because its funding was tripled. However it remains to be seen if the IMF drops its strategy of imposing structural adjustment programmes on the countries it supports, that is, demanding public sector cuts and opening the economy to global finance. Evidence of its demands on Hungary during the crisis is not hopeful. The European and US stranglehold on IMF and WTO appointments was also broken. One area of disappointment was that despite paying lip service to the idea of a 'fair and sustainable world economy', green issues barely figured. Instead there was a commitment to complete the Doha round of trade talks indicating that none of the anti-globalisation arguments had been taken on board.

By the end of 2009 the world economy was still facing decline, with unemployment rising. Public spending was coming under pressure following the huge outlays on support for the financial sector. Despite the damage that had been done there were no radical proposals to overhaul the banking and financial systems. It seemed that business as usual was likely to be the outcome. US President Obama's stimulus package was attacked because it planned to cap executive pay in bailout banks to $500,000. In anticipation, state supported banks were trying desperately to pay back government loans so that they could retain their high levels of pay and bonuses. AIG insisted on paying $165 million in bonuses even after having received a $175 billion bailout. The bonus culture, which many people saw as the main driver for excessive risk, seemed to be returning. Even the new head of the nationalised UK bank RBS negotiated a deal worth up to £10 million tied to share value. RBS also had the accolade of posting the world's worst banking loss in dollars in 2008 ($59 billion) followed by Citigroup with $53 billion. Other banks which had weathered the storm such as Goldman Sachs, were looking to pay large bonuses. One of the main justifications for the high levels of pay and bonuses was staff recruitment and retention. It seems as if the remaining parts of the financial sector were hoping to recruit or retain the person with the magic touch that could make the good times roll again. If any lessons had been learned, they were rapidly being forgotten. The lessons that should have been learned will be discussed in the next chapter.

6
LESSONS FROM THE CRISIS

We have experienced a comprehensive failure of the banking system at all levels. The banks have failed to govern themselves effectively; senior managers failed to understand the investments being made in their name; risk management and due diligence was seemingly ignored; and the non-executive directors, often eminent and hugely experienced individuals, failed in the proper scrutiny of the banks' activities. The regulatory system has also failed in its duty…This failure extends to the so-called shadow banking system which is now disintegrating before our eyes…after the extraordinary self-induced implosion of the financial system, the future of the market system now rests in the hands of governments. The politicians are the only show in town.

John McFall, Chair of the UK Treasury Select Committee
writing in a newspaper article (*Guardian* 9 January 2009)

In August 2009 writing in the same newspaper Paul Krugman agreed that it was only the return of 'big government' that had rescued western economies from depression arguing that President Obama's stimulus package had saved around a million jobs (*Guardian* 11 August 2009). Governments had not made the 1930's mistake of slashing public expenditure and cutting back money supply. Quantitative easing (government issuing new money) and other measures equivalent to nearly 15 per cent of GDP in the US and nearly 9 per cent in the UK had been authorised, although the IMF was doubtful about the outcome of the stimulus (*Financial Times* 12 August 2008). One problem was that the American term 'credit easing' rather than quantitative easing was more accurate. Most of the measures were aimed at getting bank credit rolling again and this, banks seemed very reluctant to do. Governments had poured money into their respective banking systems, but rather than being lent to local industry or householders, much of this has moved across borders as banks and financial institutions tried to settle their international commitments (Panitch and Konings 2009:82). Frustration at the failure to re-open credit lines to businesses and households produced the notable headline for an article by Philip Stevens of the *Financial Times*: 'Shoot the Bankers, nationalise the banks' (20 January 2009). The credit crunch had revealed the dilemma of attempting to finance a productive economy through capitalist finance. As capitalist businesses, banks were facing conflicting demands. They were being asked to cleanse their balance sheets and recapitalise while offering services such as essential loans to the industry and the public. The conflict between finance and productive capital became clear as leaders of industry and commerce demanded more government action to get the financial system and the wider economy moving again.

Gary Dymski sees the financial crisis in the US as resulting from 'greed and overreach by globe-spanning financial firms' (2007:1). The new methods of banking that seemed to allow bank lending to expand without limit or risk coincided with the emergence of a highly profitable, but highly risky, subprime housing market. The US's huge current account deficit had created a huge inflow of investment in government debt and into what seemed like a cast iron investment, mortgage backed securities and other debt related securities: 'for one shining moment lasting several years... participants in, and analysts of, subprime markets imagined that they were reinventing banking by creating and refining the mechanisms of structured finance' (Dymski 2007:16).

Like Cable (2009), Willem Buiter, also saw the financial crisis as a 'perfect storm' linking the new methods of securitisation, failures of rating agencies, excessive leverage, poor regulation, dis-intermediation (the emergence of new financial interconnections), poor liquidity management by the central banks and the recycling of global money through the entry of high-saving countries such as China into global trade (2009a). Ann Pettifor notes that since 2001 low income countries have been net lenders to high income countries while debt at all levels has become the 'prize legacy' of globalization (Pettifor 2006:53). This has accompanied 'anarchy in the international financial system' which 'parades as prosperity and freedom' (Pettifor 2006:146). It was inevitable that all debt would 'hit the buffers of human tolerance or the limits of the ecosystem' (Pettifor 2006:82).

Drawing on Fernand Braudel and Paul Kennedy, Phillips sees financialisation and indebtedness as a sign of imperial decline: 'financialisation has a long record of being an unhealthy late stage in the trajectory of previous leading world economic powers' (2008:viii). The financial machine had only one fuel, money itself. When no more money was forthcoming it collapsed. Even before the crisis, debt was becoming less and less effective in contributing to GDP. In the US in the 1970s for every $1 of debt there was 60 cents addition to GDP, by the early 2000s this had slumped to 20 cents (Foster and Magdoff 2009:74). Once the crisis had started, it was clear that every country that had embraced 'marketisation, deregulation and securitised finance' would get 'burned' (Mason 2009:39).

Why Did It Happen?

Central to the crisis were a debt-driven housing bubble and a bloated financial market searching for profit without taking account of underlying risk. As one Wall Street interviewee put it, 'Everyone was looking for yield. You could do almost anything you could dream of and people would buy it' (Tett 2009:35–6). Debt-fuelled investment 'leverage' was everywhere. Estimates vary, but according to Tett, in 2007 Lehman was leveraged at 29 times its actual financial resources, Merrill Lynch at x32, Goldman Sachs at x25, and Morgan Stanley and Bear Stearns at x33 (Tett 2009:172–3). Not only did banks issue huge amounts of credit, they were also borrowers and traders in credit. The financial system was a monster that was feeding itself as banks and non-banks lent and borrowed heavily and traded on the margin. Even building societies were trading in debt. Credit issue became a highly profitable business as private individuals were encouraged to 'max out' their credit cards or 'release' the inflated value of their houses. As Blackburn argues, 'financialisation encourages households to behave like businesses, businesses to behave like banks, and banks to behave like hedge funds' (2008:100). The result was hyperinflation in the financial and housing sectors (euphemistically described as capital growth) that quickly turned to bust as the huge pyramid of debt-related instruments built on the shaky foundations of financially vulnerable households collapsed. As a result, two to three million householders or their tenants are predicted to lose their homes (Blackburn 2008:98). As Japan had already shown, an over-indebted society, particularly in the context of a property boom, can leave such an overhang of debt that the whole economic structure grinds to a halt. Even then, despite economic collapse and the huge input of public funds, the reality of Wall Street socialism was denied. As the remaining private banks got up off their knees, the billions of public money that had saved them from the 'discipline' of the market were ignored. Banks such as Goldman Sachs were promising huge bonuses and even the rescued bank Merrill Lynch, which had posted losses of $27.6 billion in 2008, still sought to pay out $3.6 billion in bonuses. The danger was, as Gillian Tett has argued, that all the new liquidity provided by the state was likely to build up into another financial bubble (*Financial Times* 7 August 2009).

As capitalism goes through boom and bust cycles, there is a tendency for bank regulators to be 'behind the curve', that is, allowing bubbles to emerge by behaving pro-cyclically. Restricting money through high interest rates in reaction to inflationary threats may cause, or enhance, a slow down. Reacting to more depressed times by letting interest rates fall could stimulate a speculative surge. In the US Greenspan was widely criticised for holding interest rates too low for too long in the boom, while in Britain Mervyn King was criticised for not lowering them fast enough as the recession loomed. However the fact that Britain and the US were not co-ordinated in their approach, but both suffered similar effects in the crisis, indicates that interest rates are not effective instruments to control a runaway financial system. Equally, blame was put on the British tripartite scheme of bank regulation, but again other economies suffered with different regulation regimes. Basically, the financial system was out of control, much of it beyond the remit of regulators. Huge amounts of bank credit were being created which added to the floods of money already in circulation. States were in retreat, aided by the ideology of the Washington consensus: liberalisation, privatisation and deregulation. As Larry Elliot and Dan Atkinson argue, democratically elected governments had, over the past three decades, ceded control of the world economy to an elite of 'New Olympians' who promoted a freebooting, super-rich, globalised, unregulated capitalism (2008:5).

Given the history of financial crises in various parts of the world and the stream of bubbles that emerged in property, commodities and the dotcom boom, it is hard to understand why governments and the financial sector were so complacent about the stability of the financial system. Gillian Tett records Jerry Corrigan, a former president of the New York Federal Reserve, saying 'we knew that risk was mispriced but we did not see what was coming! I don't think anyone really did' (Tett 2009:265–6). Tett records that very few politicians or commentators showed any interest in the growing credit markets. The whole area was considered too technical and boring. At the same time the finance world showed a lack of any interest in wider social matters which, for Tett, 'cuts to the very heart of what has gone wrong' (Tett 2009:298). Financiers developed a 'silo mentality' and, locked in their little silos 'freed from external scrutiny, financiers could do almost anything they wished' (Tett 2009:299). For Tett, the impact on ordinary families of the silo mentality of financiers and the failures of the regulators 'is a damning indictment of how twenty-first-century Western society works' (Tett 2009:300).

Larry Elliot and Dan Atkinson see the regulatory failures as resulting from an almost religious 'blind faith' in capitalist markets (2008). The widespread complacency prior to the crisis appeared to be based on the assumption that the privatised financial sector had found the secret of permanent growth and prosperity. Despite tax avoidance, governments were getting considerable income from financial activities. In the UK there was a marked reluctance to tackle salaries and bonuses in the City on the grounds that the financial sector had paid £250 billion in tax since 2000. This ignores the risk to the public sector of up to £1,000 billion, with a substantial part of that being real expenditure that the financial sector has cost.

Those in the financial sector were mostly young people, mainly men, who had little sense of history and marvelled at their own cleverness. Those who were older were little wiser. The ideology of global financialised capitalism swept all before it. It was assumed that the speculators, rather than the credit system, were the creators of the wealth that seemed to be pouring out of the financial centres. Even those who were aware that the crisis was coming were unwilling to spell out the threats in case it triggered the crisis. Banks had been in serious trouble before, sometimes for years at a time, but as the public were not generally aware of this, there was no panic and the cracks were papered over (Wray 2009:12). Even when warnings were given, the timing of the actual crisis could not be predicted. Alan Greenspan warned of 'irrational exuberance' in the mid 1990s, but the dotcom crash did not happen until 1999/2000 and the financial crash was more than ten years later. While the particular timing of a crash may be difficult to predict, it is not as if there is no evidence of what can happen when financial systems get out of control.

Capitalist Finance Ignores History

In times of boom capitalism learns no lessons from history. The 2009 economic crash is eerily reminiscent of the Great Crash of 1929. That, too, saw a housing and new technology boom fuelled by consumer credit. Ordinary people became tempted by financial speculation with talk of a new economic era in which anyone, everyone, could get rich. Three million new entrants fuelled five years of stock market growth ending with a doubling of its value in 1928. Bankers' close links with the Republican politicians in power led to a laissez faire approach to the financial markets. As now, there was financial innovation and a huge amount of investment 'on the margin', that is, only putting down a small part of the share value. At the height of the speculative surge, almost half of the money borrowed was used to buy stocks and shares. No one believed the market would fall, and everyone wanted a piece of the action.

In both 1929 and 2007–08 speculative borrowing led to a financial crisis and a credit crunch. Companies went out of business because they couldn't get loans for working capital. In 1929 this led to years of depression. One major difference in 2007–08 was the immediate response of government and regulators who had learned the lessons of the 1930s when thousands of banks failed. The Great Depression produced major political changes in the post-war period, which saw strict banking and financial regulation in the US including the setting up of the Securities and Exchange Commission, the Glass Steagall Act, federal bank deposit insurance (FDIC) and the mortgage agency Fannie Mae. As the twentieth century progressed bank regulation was gradually undermined and finally formally overturned in the resurgence of market fundamentalism in the late twentieth century. The post-Depression period saw a major involvement by the US state in economic reconstruction. The Reconstruction Finance Corporation set up in 1932 invested nearly $4 trillion at today's prices and was shut down in 1946 because it was so successful it was deemed un-American (Blackburn 2008:102–3). Foster and Magdoff see finance capital as having been temporarily defeated by the Great Depression with growth capacity being taken over by the state and the military-industrial complex (2009:83). This did not defeat capitalism itself, which rebuilt its productive base with the support of the state. Then in the 1970s and 1980s finance capitalism began again to spread its wings and once more spiralled out of control (2009:72).

The problem with financialised capitalism is that there is no means of ending the process of accumulation except by a crash. In the productive economy goods and services are paid for and used, so that people need to purchase them again and again. However, money invested in money just carries on accumulating. Value piles up in assets that are truly 'fictitious' in the sense that they have no tangible basis. Financialised capital can only realise a profit if someone buys the ever appreciating asset. As a result, financial markets must suck in all possible sources of money and credit. Saul describes inflation as the 'vaporisation of money' where 'vast sums of money entered into the market place and just as quickly seemed to evaporate' (2005:140–1). Inflation in financial markets does not immediately look like evaporation. It seems as if the balloon is swelling ever larger to the benefit of all, until the crash when, like air out of a balloon, money disappears. In the stage of speculative finance capitalism, there is little to distinguish it from gambling (de Goede 2005:50). It is 'casino capitalism' where financial institutions gamble, ultimately backed by public money (Strange 1998:6). With unlimited opportunity to create credit, the privatised western banking systems kept the party going for a very long time. However, as Minsky had predicted, capitalism would fall victim to its financial instability.

The Instability of Capitalism

Hyman Minsky has been described as 'the most prolific and original theorist of financial instability' (Nesvetailova 2007:57). For Minsky, capitalism is inherently unstable and subject to credit-driven booms. At such times, capitalist financial systems will expand credit facilities despite all regulatory efforts to contain them. Following Keynes, Minsky argued that capitalist markets are not efficient and are subject to crisis through a systemic fragility. This is because financial opportunities shift and change and the viability of debt changes with them. Minsky identifies three stages in credit finance: hedge, speculative and Ponzi. For Minsky, hedge finance is relatively secure in that the investment for which the debt is raised is assumed to be profitable enough to earn sufficient return to repay the debt with interest. Speculative finance is less certain. The interest may be covered but there is not necessarily enough money to repay the capital. Ponzi is where the investment does not generate enough money to pay either the debt or the interest. In the case of housing for example, the hedge stage is when house prices are steady or rising against incomes. The speculative stage is when people are taking out interest only mortgages in the hope that future price rises or their improved financial circumstances will clear the principal debt. Ponzi is where prices are falling and/or there is insufficient money to pay any of the mortgage debt and both mortgage and interest can only be fuelled by taking on more debt.

Minsky's case is that there is always the potential for instability, particularly in periods of stability. In stable times confidence builds up and the financial system becomes more relaxed about the ability of borrowers to repay debt. If this coincides with the beginning of a bubble, speculators call forth all means of credit to join the race. Financial innovation occurs and regulators cannot keep pace with the new ways of issuing credit. Bubbles can emerge for many reasons and, once they begin, it is hard to stop the credit driven price rises that lead from speculation to Ponzi as the crisis looms (Kindleberger 1996). Speaking at a conference celebrating Minsky's ideas, McCulley argues that capitalism is intensely pro-cyclical (2008). The reality of financial markets is that while it is conventional wisdom to buy low and sell high, in practice markets do the exact opposite. No-one can believe that the good times (or the bad times) will end. When prices are high everyone wants to grab some of the profits. When prices collapse, potential investors are concerned that they will drop lower. As prices ratchet up, speculative surges lead from investments where the debt ratio to asset is low enough for both interest and loan to be easily repaid to a stage where debts are so high in relation to the asset that not even the interest can be paid. At each stage, the money invested drives up asset prices which encourages more risky behaviour until there are no new investors and the market turns down.

The Illusions of Financialisation

Phillips summarises the late twentieth and early twenty-first century as an era of:

> Bullnomics, the pied-piping of America toward a misleading financial ideology (the efficiency and reliability of markets) buttressed by a spectrum

of dubious thinkers, doctrines, and enablers: monetarist economists with their dismissal of government; economic-deregulation enthusiasts; the gurus of the Efficient Market Hypothesis, with its validation of speculators, corporate raiders, assets shuffling, debt and derivative instruments. (2008:72–73)

He goes on:

My summation...that American financial capitalism...cavalierly ventured a multiple gamble; first financializing a hitherto more diversified US economy; second, using massive quantities of debt and leverage to do so; third, following up a stock market bubble with an even larger housing and mortgage credit bubble; fourth, roughly quadrupling US credit-market debt between 1987–2007...and fifth consummating these events with a mixed performance of dishonesty, incompetence and quantitative negligence. (Phillips 2008:207)

Like Panitch and Konings, Gowan argues that there was collusion between the regulators and the investment banks in the 'new Wall Street system' (2009:20). While financial sector debt rose from 21 per cent of GDP in 1980 to 116 per cent in 2007, there was a 'global campaign to the effect that the US boom was not the result of debt-fed growth aided by highly destructive trends in the financial system, but of American free market institutions'. It was a 'bluff, buttressed by some creative national accounting practices' (Gowan 2009:25–26). Gowan claims that neither Greenspan nor Bernanke swallowed the efficient markets thesis. Both knew that the financial system was unstable and could give rise to bubbles. However, they were ready to ride the boom because of the huge amounts of 'wealth' it created on the ground and their confidence that the system they administered could cope with the crash. The clear implication of this is that the capitalist money system and the state are part of the same financial system. The financial crisis has exposed the social and political underpinnings of the financial system. The public and private sectors are intertwined. There is no such thing as a free market economy, there is a private sector supported by the public through the state. In stable times this relationship is less obvious, but a capitalist crisis, particularly a financial crisis, reveals the limitations of unregulated speculation.

Financialised capitalism has rested on the elastic creation of credit, but far from credit expansion proclaiming the dominance of speculative finance capital, it has exposed its weaknesses. It has shown that financial asset investment is always a pyramid scheme, money invested in money, whose value will collapse as soon as there are no new investors. Capitalist financial markets are as vulnerable as the productive capitalist market to the dilemma of class exploitation. Capitalism is a system built on inequality where the owners and controllers of the means of sustenance, production and money can command the labour and resources of others. Marx focused on the exploitation of workers in physical production and the primitive accumulation of primary assets such as land. However, power also comes from the ownership and control of money. States had power through their ability to issue currency and tax it back in. Capitalism has similar power through its control of financial resources. If people want to eat they have to earn money. If they cannot earn enough money they have to borrow from the same system that denies them food or sufficient wages.

Marx pointed to the contradiction of productive capitalism. If workers are not paid the full value of what they produce they do not have the money to buy the products made. Eventually the market for goods will run out and profit can no longer be realised through the money system. The same thing has happened with financialised capitalism. The financial sector has created huge differences of wealth. It sucks away money from other economic activities and the mass of the people can only hope for a trickle down of economic activity through the consumption of the champagne-swigging traders and increasing numbers of billionaires. Wider consumption is helped by debt, but again this is limited. Eventually people can borrow no more. It is not without irony that financialised capitalism fell because of its exploitation of the very poor. As capitalism runs out of a market for its goods, services or investments, all that is left is the poor. In the case of financialised capital this was the subprime householder. The subprime borrowers did not cause capitalism to fail, the cause was its own contradictions. But in this instance they were the trigger; and in that sense the poor did destroy financialised capitalism.

Financialised capitalism also misunderstood the conditions of its own existence. In the illusion that money was a neutral representation of the wealth of the market, capitalism roamed across the world seeking out the most lucrative base for low wage production, speculated on currencies and borrowed from low interest countries to invest in countries offering higher interest. In the process the financial sector grew like Topsy. The derivatives market alone was worth more than ten times world production. Financial institutions operated far and wide, well beyond their home base. This led to major problems about who should supervise their activities: the authorities in the home base, or the authorities in the branch countries? In escaping regulation and supervision, particularly in tax havens, the financialised money system was undermining its ultimate means of support. It was still a system generated by private trade and commercial borrowing and people still socially trusted its money, particularly the hard currencies. However, deregulated money had escaped from any source of legitimisation through public authority. It was also providing relatively little tax revenue to support public money. Failure to understand the real basis of the money system in the public authority of the state led banks and financial speculators to think that they were the source of money security. This led the sector to expand to such an extent that the amounts of money at risk threatened the solvency of countries. The only authority that could step in then was the International Monetary Fund (IMF) with its limited resources, given the scale of the problem. The IMF also has a pro-capitalist finance ideology that demands nation states should cut public expenditure and open themselves up to more of the same by allowing the free movement of capital. During its crisis there was popular protest in Iceland that the population should be expected to repay Holland and Britain for loans to cover the activities of Icelandic banks in those countries. The argument was that the banks were private organisations and there is no reason why the Icelandic public should be deemed responsible for private sector activities.

What Should Happen Now?

The most immediate response is more regulation, but how and on what basis? Is it enough to tackle pay and bonuses or to make banks hold more capital reserves? Should long term investors be given more power to scrutinise? Should bank directors be trained? Should there be new accounting methods, particularly for risk management? Should rating agencies, hedge funds and private equity companies be regulated? How far should the shadow banking system be regulated? Should credit derivatives and asset-based securities be formalised? Should banks be separated by function, or only allowed to grow to a particular size? What should happen to transnational banks; who should regulate them? Should banks be allowed to trade on their own account (proprietary trading)? How could the viability of the whole financial system be secured? How can bubbles be prevented? The main ideas floated on both sides of the Atlantic are for smaller, more manageable banks, formal trading for the derivative markets, getting banks to build reserves in the good times and macro-prudential regulation by the authorities to secure the viability of the whole money system. Blackburn bluntly demands that the Basle II approach to bank self-regulation of risk should be 'struck down' (2009:104). George Soros supports the need for tighter regulation, particularly higher marginal calls (how much needs to be put down to speculate on a share or other security) and minimum capital requirements against leverage, but wants to avoid 'regulatory overkill' (2008a).

When the British Prime Minister, Gordon Brown, expressed his anger at banks failing to lend despite receiving huge amounts of government support, he railed at the 'irresponsible mistakes of a few bankers'. However, the problem was much greater than a few mistakes by individuals. As George Soros has remarked 'the crisis was generated by the financial system itself' (Soros 2008a:312). Soros is an interesting poacher turned gamekeeper. He decries Thatcher and Reagan's unleashing of market forces and the fundamentalism of the Efficient Markets thesis. In his latest book, he argues that there has been a 'super-bubble' building in post-war capitalism that would inevitably collapse (2008b:81). Soros's main argument is that markets are not self-regulating but behave 'reflexively', that is, unpredictably. Therefore crisis is endemic to the financial system. It is certainly true that isolated features cannot be singled out. Although the structure of pay and bonuses has been regularly highlighted, Tony Jackson of the *Financial Times* notes that the failed US insurer AIG had long-term incentives for its staff and 30 per cent of Lehman Brothers and Bear Stearns were owned by employees. This does not mean that the high levels of pay and bonuses were justified and in August 2009 13 business school professors wrote to the *Guardian* newspaper calling for a windfall tax on bonuses to help cover the shortfall in public finances caused by the crash (12 August 2009).

For Willem Buiter, Professor of European Political Economy at the London School of Economics, a major lesson that could be learned from this 'spectacular example of market failure' is the centrality of the role of the state in the maintenance of financial stability. The financial system needs to be put back as a servant of the 'real economy', not its master. He sees the crisis as a 'great definancialisation' or a 'great deleverage' with the result that much of the financial system is effectively destroyed or exists in a state of 'subsidized limbo'. Buiter envisages a return to privatised banking but with strong regulation. He would like to see an EU-wide regulatory and fiscal authority and an end to universal banks. Buiter is concerned that this might lead to state overreach but sees this as preferable to under-regulation in the short term. However, he does not see this as a crisis for capitalism but only for 'financial capitalism' (2009b). In a later blog Buiter argues that the proposals for reform do nothing to remove the government's role as a backstop for banks. This reduces the cost to banks of ensuring against risk and allows them to grow excessively large in terms of balance sheets and leverage. Even though the financial sector accounts for only 8 per cent of GDP in the UK, its potential impact is very high as has been seen. Buiter's answer is to remove the guarantee that underpins banks. No public money should be put into banks unless all creditors are converted into shareholders and thus threatened by bank collapse. Banks are not only too large, but they are hard to regulate and tax because they operate across borders. The problem now is that banks operate internationally but still have a national backup (Buiter 2009c).

Strong support for at least temporary nationalisation has come from economists such as Paul Krugman, Joseph Stiglitz, Willem Buiter and Nouriel Roubini. This is supported by John McFall, Chair of the UK Treasury Select Committee, who has called for the establishment of a state bank to deliver government lending targets and who notes that after World War II the Labour government, led by Attlee, directed bank lending (*Guardian* 9 January 2009). Professor Nouriel Roubini, of the Stern Business School at the University of New York, wants bad banks set up to take on the toxic assets and temporary nationalisation of troubled banks. He argues that this will be cheaper and better than governments supporting 'zombie' banks. Joseph Stiglitz writing in the *Herald Tribune* (2 April 2009) agrees that hurling billions of public money at banks is far worse than nationalising, as it is privatising gains while socialising losses. He sees this also applying to the setting up of a 'bad bank' that would relieve the private sector of its bad assets. There is also the difficulty of the price that the state would pay for those assets. Roubini argues that after the banks have been 'cleaned up' they should be returned to the private sector. He points out this has already been achieved for one of the early failures, California-based Indymac. He also calls for financial help for the wider economy particularly for mortgage-holders (CNNMoney 2009). Even before the crisis, Roubini countered Greenspan's argument that there was no case for a federal reserve response to asset bubbles such as dotcom, the important thing was to deal with the aftermath of bursting bubbles. Roubini argued that central banks need to be even handed and respond to the rise of bubbles, as well as the collapse, otherwise there will be distorted and perverse incentives, economic imbalance and a low savings rate (2006:105).

Many of the suggestions for the future of banking envisage the continuation of privatised finance but with better regulation. A major aim is to make banks small enough to fail, or to insulate consumer retail banking from investment finance. It is questionable whether a banking system based on the pursuit of profit could ever separate retail banking services from speculative investment. It was pressure from retail banks that saw Glass Steagall repealed. Northern Rock did not have an investment arm, yet was still brought down through its trading connections to the investment sector. Lehman was not a retail bank, but its collapse impacted on high street banks. The privatised financial system is one network. The financial collapse was not a failure of cheats, rogues and Gordon Gekkos who, like his character from the 1987 film 'Wall Street', declared that greed was good; it was the systematic failure of a capitalist money system driven by the search for profit. As Minsky argued, finance capitalism will always search for innovative ways of raising credit to speculate. McCulley agrees that it is difficult to separate the 'real' banking system from the shadow banking system. The US state tried to step back and let Lehman fail, but within days had to rescue AIG. McCulley argues that since the rescue of Bear Stearns, the whole shadow banking system has come under the state's liquidity umbrella (2008). Mason also argues that the collapse of Lehman was a 'harbinger of the changing power balance in the world-from banks to states' (Mason 2009:3). However, this also meant that 'moral hazard is back on an unthinkable and explicit scale' if every money-market investor and every bank knows it will be rescued by the state. As Mason points out, the whole testosterone driven mayhem on the trading floors was always a con, 'there was always a safety net. The giants of the financial system could gamble, lose everything, and yet walk away solvent' (Mason 2009:21).

The privatised issue of credit money through the banking system has led to speculation on a massive scale which has now fallen on state authority to rescue. The state has not been able to let the market take its course and 'cleanse' itself, as it has proved impossible to separate out pure speculation from people's personal savings, particularly those institutionalised through pensions and other long term investment. The financialisation of substantial numbers of the general public has muddied the waters of financialised capitalism. The public is therefore implicated in two ways, both as financialised savers and investors and as tax payers. Although banks had been subject to light touch regulation, they were still a regulated financial sector. They were linked to the government through the central bank and it was clear that governments could not let their banks fail. However, as the failure of the liquidity mechanisms showed, the problems in the banking system were much deeper than the failure of money and credit to circulate. Banks weren't just suffering a problem of liquidity, they were effectively insolvent despite their reserves.

Claude Hillinger puts forward an approach that would see the state guarantee all bank deposits while letting the private or public companies running the banks fail (2008:308). Soros argues against this, pointing out that peripheral countries have suffered very badly when stronger economies have guaranteed their deposits as savings have flooded from the periphery towards the centre. As a result, peripheral countries have had to keep their interest rates very high (Soros 2008a:313). Soros's criticism assumes that money would still be able to flow freely around the world and that reform would only take place in one country. Hillinger's proposal is a way forward that governments have implicitly or explicitly taken. All savings have been guaranteed, even where there are deposit insurance limits. The question is what happens after the banks fail? The logic would be a national savings system and a national bank. There would be unlimited moral hazard if profit seeking banks were able to continue with a 100 per cent deposit guarantee, even if the punishment for misbehaviour would be company failure.

McCulley points to a structural problem facing the banking system. Like Keynes' paradox of thrift, where the economy does not function if everyone saves, in the present situation the whole economy cannot de-lever at the same time. Keynes' solution was to run deficits using public money and for McCulley the solution to de-levering is the same: use the sovereign's (i.e. the state's) balance sheet. If the private sector wants to shrink, a depression can only be avoided if someone takes up the slack and that has to be the state's money creation role. As McCulley points out, 'that someone is the guy who owns a printing press and is allowed to print legal tender and who gets his ink for free. That happens to be, in a most direct sense, my dear friend Ben Bernanke. But in a broader sense, it's the sovereign' (McCulley 2008). As Gowan argues, it is an illusion to think that regulation can replace the centrality of the state to the stability of a financial system. The globalised financial system is inherently unstable because the state cannot play its underpinning role through 'tax-raising capacity and currency printing presses' (Gowan 2009:23).

Another illusion of the capitalist financial sector is that credit-driven capitalism is compatible with the delivery of banking services to the mass of the population. As discussed in Chapter 2, banking is an inherently unstable system. The essence of all deposit-based banking is to 'borrow' short and lend long, thus always threatening problems of liquidity or solvency. The only immediate safeguard is the amount of reserves a bank holds and these can be as low as 0.1 per cent as D'Arista pointed out (2008). The level of reserves becomes even more important if the bank has itself borrowed in order to lend. In a profit-driven banking system, the aim must be to hold as little reserve as possible because it is 'dead money' earning no profit, and to maximise loans, or to engage in financial activities that bring in a profit. However, even a high level of reserve, such as 10–12 per cent, would be of little use in a crisis. For a crisis the only effective reserve for deposits, as government action has shown, is 100 per cent. This would undermine the key factor in the growth and expansion of economies under the modern banking system, the absence of any direct link between deposits and lending. Borrowing short and lending long, together with the fractional reserve system, has been the whole basis of the money creation system of capitalism. Such an illogical system always threatened crises of liquidity, or in the case of the current crisis, insolvency. To completely eliminate 'fresh air' lending and to directly tie savers to borrowers would dramatically slow down the economy.

In the search for profit, the more lending or other forms of financial activity a bank engages in, the more likely it is that it will lose money and not be able to meet its liabilities (that is pay back the bank's own borrowings, honour agreed loans to customers or give people back their savings). The aim of the Glass Steagall legislation was to separate the savings of depositors from the more risky operations of the financial markets. It is this barrier that the deregulated financial system broke down. Banks started to get involved in financial speculation, not only as a lender to speculators, but speculating with their own reserves. All of this followed the logic of the search for profit. In the good times banks produced good returns and rode high in the stock market. The financial spiral twisted around as institutional investors started to see banks as a safe investment. Shareholders wanted to see higher dividends and capital growth and this drove the banks to take more risks. The clear lesson is that securing people's savings is not compatible with operating as a profit-driven business. As banking systems are inherently unstable and the services they give are vital for economic functioning, 'public ownership of the credit and banking system is rational and, indeed, necessary along with democratic control' (Gowan 2009:2). Blackburn offers a compromise where states should be allocated shares in banks to compensate for their financial contribution. Banks would also make an allocation to a social fund (Blackburn 2008:102). However, this assumes that banks still retain their money creating powers.

It is the money creation power of banks that is the essential question. As Pettifor argues, 'the invention of bank money – money that did not depend on existing economic activity, but *created* economic activity – meant that borrowers could end their dependency on those who were already rich...bank money widened and democratized the allocation of credit' (Pettifor 2006:67). However, if the logic of loans follows the capitalist notion of profit, the democratic potential of money will be lost, and this is what has happened. Pettifor sees banking as a 'parasitic sector' charging interest on loans meaning that further new money must be found, either by increased productive or commercial activity, or by someone else taking out new debt (2006:19). However, it is the public and democratic nature of money that is the most important issue: 'because it is created by society, money is actually the property of society...and should not therefore be appropriated by banks as their sole property' (Pettifor 2006:176). Pettifor's solution is free government money, cheap commercial money and regulated credit creation. Parenteau (2008) has argued that there are only three ways forward from the current 'age of financialisation'. One is to continue to live in a 'Ponzi Nation', that is, to let the current under-regulated system operate and accept that problems of fraud and speculation will occur. The second approach is to impose a regulation system that is 'Glass–Steagall on Stilts'. The third is to look at wider reforms of the financial system. It would be a tragedy if public money was used to put the capitalist Humpty Dumpty back together again.

Conclusion

The financial crisis presents an historic moment to put forward radical alternatives. The need for state intervention has exposed the contradictions of financialised capitalism and its reliance on 'Wall Street socialism'. A pivotal point was the rescue of the US investment bank, Bear Stearns; the state was not only bailing out commercial banks, but finance capital as well. This clearly exposed the fact that the failure to exercise democratic control over money issue has meant the benefits of the money system have been privatised, while the risks have been socialised. Those who lend and borrow the money that is created out of 'nowhere' are using a social and public resource for private gain. They are creating claims upon society that are ultimately guaranteed only by society itself, but this is being used for private profit, not public benefit. Financial speculators are not being entrepreneurial by 'making' money, they are using money to create more money in a cycle that must end in failure as there is no value-creating source other than the money system itself. This is the moment to ask if another way is possible. Can the money system be organised in such a way that it does not revert to financial speculation? Can a money system be devised that can meet the provisioning needs of human societies in a flexible way that does not encourage capital accumulation, the exploitation of people or the degradation of the environment? The financial crisis has created an historic moment when 'those who want to impose social justice and sustainability on globalised capitalism have a once-in-a lifetime chance' (Mason 2009:x). The next chapter will discuss ways in which that chance might be taken.

7

PUBLIC MONEY AND SUFFICIENCY PROVISIONING

The history of the emergence of modern money has seen shifting control between public authorities and the capitalist market. While many states were dependent upon loans from capitalist bankers and financiers, until the latter part of the twentieth century most states still regulated, and even directed, the private banking sector, controlled the cross border movement of money and issued notes and coin. The globalisation of finance and the shift away from the use of notes and coin to debt-based money issue, led to dominance of the money system by a profit-driven banking and financial sector. Under the banner of neo-liberalism, money issue and circulation was put almost exclusively under the control of capitalist market forces through substantial bank deregulation and the growth of a large unregulated financial sector. As old-fashioned banking and mutual societies floundered, there emerged a panoply of financial activities that drew high street banks and non-bank financial agencies into an unholy alliance of credit creation and speculation. The state was 'rolled back' together with mutualism and any possibility of recognising money as public or social.

The era of market fundamentalism was led by the Anglo–American economies with the enthusiastic support of their states. The financial markets appeared to be a source of unlimited wealth with public expenditure and tax-raising seen as an imposition on the capitalist 'wealth creators'. State regulation of the money system was reduced to merely a concern with inflation, certainly in Britain. This meant that as the crisis arose the British monitoring authorities were looking the wrong way. The financial crisis has shown how fragile the money system is under the control of profit-driven market forces. The failure of one of the free market's core mechanisms, the elastic creation of money as debt, revealed the shallow nature of private control and the ultimate reliance of the whole structure of financialised capital on the financial capacity of the state. The strutting claims of the economic superiority of the capitalist market with all its social, economic and environmental destructiveness, was seen to be a charade. If the destructiveness of privatised money is not to recur it is important to open a debate about the future of money and how it can be used in more socially and ecologically sustainable ways.

Far from being a natural and neutral adjunct to the market, money has proved to be a profoundly social and political institution. As such, the way money is issued, circulated and controlled should be subject to critical analysis. A discussion of the future of money must not only draw lessons from the latest financial crisis, but from the structure of the financial system as a whole. This includes the way that money is defined and operates within the economy and the ownership and control of the money system in its various levels and manifestations. Failure to do this will mean returning to some version of business as usual, until the next crisis. The opportunity to develop a money system that can help human societies achieve a more socially just and ecologically sustainable form of provisioning will be missed. This does not mean starting from scratch. It is already clear that the money system is a purely social phenomenon with no 'natural' basis for valuing human activities. Nor can money systems operate autonomously or spontaneously: they are essentially social and public, requiring prior systems of trust and authority. Money does not create society, society creates money. What is important is how money is owned and controlled. Like conventional economists, most radical economists have seen the role of money as marginal to their analysis. Conventional economics, taking its ideological framework from capitalist domination of production and exchange, ignored the social and political underpinnings of money and tied its analysis of the origins and function of money to the market system. This ignored the public responsibility and public interest inherent in the issue and circulation of money. As argued in Chapter 1, all money is a credit or claim on the resources or output of human societies. The control of money issue and circulation, therefore, has implications for everyone connected to that money system. Money is a social phenomenon and a public resource, but, with the collusion of the state, it has been harnessed for the benefit of a privileged few.

Creating a Socially Just 'Sufficiency' Economy

A major criticism of the debt-based capitalist system is that it demands continual expansion. People are urged to constantly produce, consume and borrow in order to create profit (Lawson 2009). From a green perspective 'sustainability requires a money supply system that can run satisfactorily if growth stops' (Douthwaite 1999:27). The economic system should be able to provision human society on an equitable basis without destructive growth. Central to this would be the ideas of sufficiency and social justice. Sufficiency would mean providing enough goods and services to maintain a good quality of life. Social justice would mean that the money system would need to ensure that economic priorities would be determined in the interests of the most vulnerable members of the community. A key development in the emergence of capitalism was the erection of the barrier of private property between humans and their means of sustenance. At first this was policed by force and tradition, but money and waged labour have proved to be a much more flexible means of accumulation of wealth for those who own the means of production and sustenance, particularly when they could control the issue and circulation of money as well (Hutchinson et al. 2002:70).

For those who do not have direct access to resources or money, the only means of sustaining themselves is to sell their labour. In order to consume, money must be earned. Those employed are expected to be grateful to the owners of resources and money for the gift of employment. As well as leading to exploitation and inequality, waged labour for profit creates a destructive distance between the work people do and their immediate needs. The provisioning of necessities and public services has to piggy-back on profit-driven activities, extracting reluctantly paid taxes or other contributions to public welfare. Provisioning in a capitalist economy based on waged labour is a two-step rather than a one-step process. Work is not undertaken directly for social benefit but to maximise profit, that is, to enable capital accumulation. Inequality of access to money means that economic demand is biased towards the wealthy and discretionary expenditure. It is geared to meeting the wants of the rich, not the needs of the poor. There is no mechanism for society as a whole to express its needs on an egalitarian basis, or to allow for sufficiency-based provisioning.

From a green perspective, the growth dynamic of capitalism is destructive of the natural world. Its drive endlessly to invest capital in new ventures produces social and environmental consequences that demand a different type of economics (Scott Cato 2009). Green economists argue that nature is a 'real-real' economy with physical and biological limits that extends far beyond the market notion of the 'real' economy. The 'growth as progress' dynamic of the capitalist model must eventually push up against the capacity of the environment to sustain human activity (Kallis et al. 2009:16–18). O'Connor sees this as a 'second contradiction' for capitalism. The first is the traditional Marxian problem of economic crisis, the second is that capitalism's activities are destroying the social and environmental conditions of its own existence (1996). As Perelman warns, while 'the financial system can bail out a Long Term Capital Management for a few billion dollars... nobody knows how to recover depleted energy sources or to rescue devastated environments on a global scale' (2003:93).

Green economics is a broad church that runs from market solutions to the small scale Buddhist economics of Schumacher's 'right livelihood' (1973:44). Market oriented proposals seek to temper the 'bottom line' of financial profitability through measures such as environmental accounting, assessments and audits to various proposals for green taxes or tradable pollution permits.

The example of the EU Emissions Trading Scheme indicates that the market system is not a suitable medium for addressing environmental problems. A generous number of tradable carbon credits were issued just before the recession began. These were cashed in by firms who felt they didn't need them, which forced down the price of carbon, making alternative energy schemes seem very expensive. The alternative to carbon trading could be a steep carbon tax or regulation and restriction of use. However, within a global capitalist economy a more restrictive solution might only produce a 'race to the bottom' as production shifted to countries with the lowest tax and least regulation. For Joan Martinez-Alier, a leading ecological economist, the values of a profit-driven market system are incommensurable with the values of ecological sustainability (1987). This view was shared by the early twentieth-century Scottish scientist Frederick Soddy. He saw people as so besotted with token-money and the virtual wealth of paper money that they did not pay attention to the real damage and poverty that surrounded them. His particular concern was the exploitation of fossil fuel. As all human activities depended upon energy there would be future impoverishment when supplies ran out (Merricks 1996). The question of the balance between ecology and economy was reinvigorated in the early 1970s by Nicholas Georgescu-Roegen (1971) and Herman Daly (1973) and launched the search for an alternative ecological economics.

Despite the limitations of a market response to environmental problems, there is halting mainstream recognition that the green warnings are real, particularly in terms of climate change. The idea of a 'Green New Deal' producing jobs through green technology and environmental protection has been put forward on both sides of the Atlantic. An independent Sustainable Development Commission, set up by the UK government, produced a report that challenged the link between prosperity and growth in 2009. The report rejected a capitalist market solution to inequality and ecological sustainability as simplistic, 'assumptions that capitalism's propensity for efficiency will allow us to stabilise the climate and protect against resource scarcity are nothing short of delusional' (Jackson 2009:7). The report sees the financial crisis as largely triggered by the growth imperative as continued expansion of credit was deliberately courted as an essential mechanism to stimulate consumption and growth. The period of financialisation, far from spreading prosperity, markedly increased inequality while wealth 'trickled up to the lucky few' (Jackson 2009:6). Growth, in any case, is unsustainable. To enable the global population to live at the level of the OECD countries, the global economy would need to be 40 times larger by the end of the century.

The report is ambivalent about the idea of a Keynesian stimulus through a Green New Deal. While seeing it as an 'eminently sensible' response to the economic crisis, it does not solve the overall problem if economies then return to business as usual. The report praises Herman Daly's work on the notion of a 'steady state economy' which would conserve physical resources, but points out that there is no viable macroeconomic model to achieve this. It concludes by calling for an economics that abandons the presumption of growth in material consumption as the basis of economic stability. What is needed is an economics that is 'ecologically and socially literate, ending the folly of separating economy from society and environment' (Jackson 2009:10). It remains to be seen how far the British or American economies will embrace the Green New Deal, let alone an alternative economics.

The report is not right in saying there is no macroeconomics based on integrating economy, society and environment. Certainly there is not one in the mainstream, but ideas are emerging through heterodox frameworks. One is ecofeminist political economy, which sees gender as the key to the separation of the economy from society and the environment (Mellor 2009, Perkins and Kuiper 2005, Hutchinson et al. 2002). Ecofeminist political economy argues that women's work and lives form the missing link between economy and nature. The capitalist market is disembodied and disembedded, carved out of the totality of human existence within the natural world. Seeing the capitalist market as socially disembedded is not new, it was argued by Polanyi (1944), but ecofeminists see it as more materially disembedded from the human body and the natural world. This is because it is not just capitalism that puts a monetary boundary around the activities that it sees as profitable, patriarchy puts a monetary boundary around what work is considered worthy of payment. Much of women's work and lives lies outside these boundaries as unpaid or low paid work. What is important about this excluded or marginalised work is that it is the work of the body in relation to human frailty and the human life cycle; work that is concerned with the young, the old, the sick, the unhappy, that is, care in its broadest sense.

The exclusion from money value of domestic and communal work around human mental and physical existence is akin to the way capitalist patriarchy externalises the natural world. The resilience of the natural world, like caring work, is treated as a free resource. This does not imply an essential difference between men and women. Many women hold privileged positions within the money-framed economy, while men can be involved in unpaid care or community work. The mechanism is a material one, the money-framed economy can operate as it does because it can exploit the unpaid, or underpaid, caring work that is mainly done by women, together with the resources of the natural world. Ignoring or marginalising the needs of the human body with its frailties enables the illusion of an independently functioning 'Economic Man' (Mellor 1997). 'His' money-based life ignores the embodied-ness of human life and the embedded-ness of humanity in the natural environment. 'Economic Man' is not young or old, sick or unhappy and does not have pressing domestic demands that cannot be ignored or put off. Thus, the artificial boundary of human activities that is called the 'economy' fails to acknowledge its true resource base and the parasitical way it is sustained by systems of unpaid social labour and the resources and resilience of the natural environment (Bennholdt-Thomsen and Mies 1999:31, Hutchinson et al. 2002:180). As a result these are exploited and damaged. It is the fragility of human existence that is the link to the fragility of the natural environment. This fragility is what lies beyond the boundary of the money economy.

Ecofeminist political economy challenges the exploitative boundaries of the economy as defined by capitalist patriarchy (Mies 1999:37). It seeks to create a provisioning system that can meet human needs and enhance human potential without destroying the life of the planet. A provisioning economy would start from the embodiment and embedded-ness of human lives, human well-being and the vitality of the natural world. Such an emphasis would mean that patterns of work and consumption would be sensitive to the human life cycle and the replenishing needs of the planet. The provisioning of necessary goods and services would be the main focus of the economy and the activities of production and exchange would be fully integrated with the dynamics of the body and the environment. A money system for such an economy would need to embrace this wider notion of provisioning. It would need to enable the building of a non-gendered, egalitarian and ecologically sustainable provisioning economy. It would therefore need to prioritise these needs and this work in the issue of money. Money would be brought back from the capitalist market and re-united with its social and public base.

Given that money emerges by fiat, out of 'fresh air', whether it takes the form of metal, paper or a sight bank account, it is not created by the mental or manual labour of any particular group in society. It is brought into being through a combination of private, public and social acts. Far from reflecting the labour of the actual issuer, money is produced as a claim for resources and labour. There is no reason why these claims should be harnessed for the personal benefit of the issuer. As something that is produced without specific labour, the social resource of money is akin to a natural resource. Like natural resources, money can be seen as subject to individual property rights or as a Commons, that is, something that is not owned by any individual or group, but is a 'Common Wealth', for the benefit of all (Large 2010). Commons resources are those which should 'belong' to the people as a whole, and in the case of the natural environment to the non-human world as well. If they are 'used' at all Commons resources should be for the benefit of all. Capitalism has been built on the privatisation of Commons resources (Scott Cato 2006:156–7). Land and other resources have been expropriated or enclosed by private ownership through the expulsion of inhabitants, or the removal of their rights to use previously common land.

Historically this grab of assets was often achieved by force, but money is even more effective. Privately 'enclosed' money is used to buy resources and productive assets in the same way that colonists bought Manhattan for strings of beads (wampum was valued money in the area at the time). Privatisation of the social resource of money is central to capitalism; if a provisioning sufficiency economy is to be achieved, money must be reclaimed for the benefit of the people as a whole. It must be reclaimed as public money and brought under democratic control. This is not such an impossible task as it seems, given that the privatisation of money is an illusion anyway.

The Public Foundations of Private Money

The analysis of money presented in this book has shown that the privatisation of money is an illusion, as the only mechanism that can guarantee the security of the money system is the public authority of the state. Money also represents mechanisms of social trust. However, through the dominance of capitalist neo-liberal ideology the operation of the money system has been privatised. The market driven 'democratisation' of finance has presented the capitalist market as the people's friend and the public sector as the enemy. There is very little popular support for the public sector, read as the state, and its expenditure, as people have been encouraged to think that the state is a drain on the 'real' economy and the money in their pockets. However, this 'real' economy only represents the profit driven interests of the patriarchal capitalist market. Debt-driven finance lives off the promise of the continued future circulation of money which ultimately needs the backing of the state and its taxation mechanisms. Despite the fact that the money system depends on social trust and public authority, the most important power of money, the ability to create it, has been given away to the private sector. The first step, therefore, must be to reclaim money creation for the Commons, for the people as a whole (Harmer 1999, Daly 1999, Douthwaite 1999, Robertson 1998, Rowbotham 1998, Robertson and Bunzl 2003, Huber and Robertson 1999, Scott Cato 2009). As Bernard Lietaer has argued, 'money is too important to be left only to bankers and economists' (preface to Douthwaite 1999:6–7).

To remove its capacity to create money would be to destroy the basis of the modern banking system. As has been argued, the principle of borrowing short and lending long means that all loans are an act of money creation. To the extent that they operate on the same principle, all mutual savings and loans organisations are also creating money. However, for those under strict regulation or democratic control, there are limits to the amount of loans that can be issued or the use to which they can be put. Financialised capitalism exposed the unlimited powers of money creation held by the commercial banks and showed the way in which it could be abused for the benefit of a very rich minority while drowning much of the rest of society in debt. If money creation was returned to the public to determine, commercial banks would no longer be able to create new credit. Instead, they would adopt the role that they are commonly assumed to hold, as credit-broking financial intermediaries. Money invested could not be withdrawn until sufficient debt was repaid. People who lent their money would know it was at risk. Leverage would also be much more difficult to obtain with no mechanism of money creation. The economy would have to operate on much more steady state principles, as the debt dynamic for growth would be truncated.

Public responsibility for securing the financial system has been made transparent during the financial crisis and this has enabled the case for returning money creation to the public to move closer to the mainstream. In January 2009 US Congressman Dennis Kucinich put forward the case for monetary reform arguing that with 10 million Americans already out of work and heading for 12 million, the time had come for Congress to reclaim control of the money system. The retort by supporters of the capitalist market will be that the state would be inefficient in allocating money. Given the extraordinary behaviour of the financial markets, it would seem the efficient market thesis has no credibility in this regard. However, this will not be widely understood unless radical thinkers take the problem of Wall Street socialism seriously. It is not just a case of emergency support for the financial system. The public always stands in support of its legal tender. As became clear in the financial crisis, public support is not limited to regulated banks: it extends to the whole of private finance. This was shown when the US state stepped in to support Bear Stearns and was demonstrated even more forcefully when the state's failure to support Lehman nearly brought down the whole banking system. No matter what firewalls are put up, it is not possible to separate profit-driven financial institutions, or the ebbs and flows of profit-seeking finance, from high street deposits. While the money system remains the creature of capitalist finance, the public will be responsible for its survival. Wall Street socialism is therefore not an aberration: it is how the money system is constructed. The notion of private finance is a sham. Privatised money exists by courtesy of the state and the wider public who hosts it.

The principle must be that if the public, via the state, stands guarantee for the capitalist financial system, then that system must be in public hands. Under neo-liberal ideology the notion of the state has been almost entirely separated from the notion of the public good. However it is important not to just reverse the neo-liberal argument: private bad, public good. States have been major promoters of privatised finance. Public authorities would not necessarily use money wisely, unless they were subject to democratically-based mandates and public scrutiny. If money is to be democratised, the priorities of the state need to be determined by the wider public. Public authorities must be clear that their loyalties must rest with the public as a whole. For this to happen it must be made clear that the capitalist sector has no mechanism for ensuring the public good. Its aim of wealth creation is not for the benefit of the public, but is at the expense of the public, nationally and internationally. It is driven by the need to make profit in whatever way possible. The capitalist market has globally brought goods and services to the billion or so better off, but cannot provision the world's people on a socially just or ecologically sustainable basis. Individual capitalists may also indulge in philanthropy but there are at least two problems with this. First, they are directly or indirectly using the privatised capacity for debt-based money creation to fuel their financial accumulation, money which could have been issued by the public for public good. Second, the priorities for philanthropic expenditure reflect the whim of the donor, not the democratically identified needs of the people.

A great deal of waste and unnecessary production and consumption would be avoided if public services could be paid for directly through money issue. Rather than debt-based money being created and circulated through the market, money creation could be achieved through the provision of socially necessary work and then flow outward towards the market. At present, given that money is issued largely into the private sector, it has to be taxed back out again (with difficulty) for public use. Socially-issued money would go the other way round, prioritising democratically determined socially relevant expenditure with the commercial economy having to earn the money into its sector through carrying out socially relevant and ecologically sustainable activities. Beneficial expenditure would have first call on money issue with the capitalist market (to the extent it continued to exist) offering goods and services to attract that money as it circulated. In such a system, people would have much more opportunity to work in areas that directly affected their lives. The two-step economy of alienated work would become a one-step integration of work and needs. The vital question is, how would the one-step economy operate? Richard Douthwaite, in his analysis of the 'ecology of money', argues that there are three ways in which money can be created, through commercial activities, through public authority and through socially generated money (1999:11).

Socially Produced Money

There are broadly two ways in which social money can be created: through the issue and circulation of a local currency or through an accounting system based on membership of a trading group. Social money systems tend to be locally based with the aim of building a local economy. The best known examples of schemes that rely on membership and accounting, rather than a tangible currency, are LETS (Local Exchange Trading Systems) devised by a Canadian, Michael Linton, in the early 1980s. LETS are membership organisations where people carry out tasks or trade with each other with a record of debits and credits kept in a notional currency of account (Raddon 2003, North 2007). The alternative is to issue a local currency. A well-recorded example is in the small university town of Ithaca in New York state. Currency notes, 'Ithaca Hours', are denominated by time, from quarter-hour to two-hour, valued at the national average hourly rate. The 'Ithaca Hours' are issued as loans or grants to charities, or payments to those who advertise in the movements' directory, and are accepted by many local businesses. The founder was inspired by the example of the British co-operative pioneer Robert Owen's National Equitable Labour Exchange scheme of 1832–34 (Raddon 2003:13). Another well-known and widespread example is the Time Dollar system devised by Edgar Cahn, a US Professor and Civil Rights Lawyer. Time dollars are earned by giving a timed service to another person, but there is no money equivalence. In Japan Hureai Kippu (caring relationship tickets) are used for care of the elderly (Douthwaite 1999:5). Care-givers can accumulate health care credits for their own use, or they can transfer their credit to others, for example to obtain care for relatives living in another part of the country.

Alternative or complementary currencies often emerge in times of economic stress, most notably in the 1930s. In 1932, Michael Unterguggenberger the mayor of Worgl in Austria, facing the unemployment of one-third of his small town, issued around 10,000 schillings in scrip notes (scrip is privately-issued money that does not qualify as legal tender). Following the principles of Silvio Gesell (1862–1930) the scrip was subject to demurrage, that is, to maintain its value it had to be stamped for a small fee each month, an encouragement to spend it quickly. The money was used to pay the wages of city employees and for public works. It was also accepted in payment of local taxes. The scrip money was a great success, circulating much more quickly than the national currency and unemployment fell by 25 per cent (Douthwaite and Wagman 1999:97). Douthwaite and Wagman see the issue of 'auxiliary currencies' as 'an important step in the democratisation of money creation' (1999:6). This was a view shared by the Austrian government who declared the scheme illegal. The US government in the 1930s also closed down several hundred similar money systems, fearing that the US monetary system was being 'democratised out of its hands' (1999:100).

Local money systems are favoured by green activists and economists as a means of building a local economy (Scott Cato 2006:131–2). As Woodin and Lucas argue, local money systems can boost resilience in local economies. They can promote economic solidarity, provide alternative liquidity, supply low cost finance to local businesses and retain wealth within the local area (2004:195). There are, however, limitations to local money or trading systems. Mostly they are very small particularly if, like LETS, they work on face-to-face interactions with records kept of each interaction. North, in a wide ranging survey of local trading systems, comes to some pessimistic conclusions. To claims that non-capitalist local markets can be organised he points out that 'advocates of alternative practices ignore the extent to which such practices have been tried before, always ending in shipwreck' (North 2007:174). His case is that such schemes cannot escape the capitalist market. Money creation itself is not enough. Access to basic resources is needed and this requires access to mainstream money. A local money system can only harness those resources and activities it controls (North 2007:178). It is not the creation of money that is important but the breadth of its recognition. In the absence of public authority, social money can only rely on the trust and fairness of the people within the system. People who promote the idea of local money often see local currencies as one among many, ranging from the local to the global. Richard Douthwaite sees room for four currencies: national, international, local and a special currency for savings (1999:53).

While social money initiatives are often small scale, they can provide the flexibility to allow communities to explore alternative ways of provisioning their needs and structuring their lives. They offer 'glimmers of spaces beyond or outside capitalism' (Gibson-Graham 1996:88). The British consumer co-operative movement shows that large scale organisation enabling widespread economic

What do 'big' men do in small localities?

change can emerge from small local initiatives (Mellor et al. 1988:15–17). Starting from a group of weavers in Rochdale in 1844, putting aside sixpence a week to collectively buy a bag of flour to sell among themselves, it grew within a generation to a 'cradle to grave' supply chain for the working class of Britain. Consumer co-operatives met the needs of a substantial part of the British working class population by the post-war period with shops, factories, farms and funeral parlours. In the twenty-first century it remains the country's biggest farmer. Its bank, insurance society and building society (now independent as the Nationwide) flourish. It did not launch a new currency, but it was an alternative production and trading system that dominated working class provisioning until the private sector used its financial muscle to enter the food market and launch the wider consumer society.

In complex societies it is clear that a public money system is needed to enable production and exchange. People need to be issued with 'credit' to start the process. This does not necessarily have to be issued as debt. Money could be issued directly to launch the production process, particularly if goods and services were to be provided on a not-for-profit basis. If production and consumption is to be as close to sufficiency as possible, people should be able to directly produce the goods and services they need. At present money creation is fed through a profit-driven capitalist market whose aim is not to provision society, but to create a profit. Capitalism has harnessed the production of money to feed its own accumulation of wealth. It is a system driven by consumption and growth. It can never be the basis of a sufficiency society, or one that is economically just. The aim must be to redirect the money system so that people can collectively provision themselves within ecological constraints.

Making Money Public

One of the problems the state has faced as the modern money system developed was that it became indebted to the commercial sector. In giving away its money creation capacity, as bank debt took over from note and coin issue, the need to borrow

In a perfectly regulated economy how do you accommodate the original entrepreneur?

money became even more pressing. As capitalist ideology moved heavily against the public sector having any money creation capacity, the only sources of money for the state were unpopular: taxes and borrowing. Even when the British state did engage in quantitative easing, that is, money creation, the opposition and media commentators generally persisted in referring to the problem of debt that was being foisted on future generations. No distinction appeared to be made between government borrowing and money creation.

If money issue was returned to public control, it could be used directly by the state and local authorities for necessary public expenditure social benefit. However making money creation public need not mean making it subject to state control. Money could be issued in various ways. Publicly-issued credit could be made available to co-operatives, mutuals or other types of social businesses or to carefully regulated private businesses to deliver public goods. Alternatively, a citizen's income could be provided which would emerge into the economy as a demand for goods and services (Lord 1999). As a universal payment, a citizen's income would remove the stigma of being 'on benefit' and could support more creative work, education or community activity, as well as providing an income for those doing unpaid caring work. The level of such an income could also be enhanced to help balance an economy. For example, extra payments could be paid to people who live or settle in under-populated regions or paid to support populations with particular difficulties, or people who undertake particular tasks such as caring.

Public money issue could also be openly used for social incomes such as pensions. As Wray points out, this is what happens now through the social security system: 'let us stop pretending, and recognise Social Security promises for what they are – that is, commitments by a sovereign government to credit bank accounts on schedule' (2009:16).

To avoid politicians using money creation in their own interests, as bankers have done, Huber and Robertson suggest that the level of new money issue should be determined by monetary authorities, operationally independent as the Bank of England

This § col be greatly expanded psychologically.
The press. advertising. spin.

now is, but accountable to elected governments for achieving their published, democratically approved monetary objectives (2000:15). The monetary authorities would give the new money they create to the government as public revenue to be spent into circulation for public purposes under an accepted democratic budgetary procedure.

The most important change must be democratic input into economic priorities. It may be questioned whether people would be able to make detailed democratic decisions on financial matters. It would not be envisaged that the public would engage in detailed decision-making. The most important thing would be to indicate provisioning priorities that the financial system would follow. This is the basis of participatory budgeting (Nylen 2003) most notably in Porto Alegre in Brazil, but copied elsewhere (Albert 2003:15). People already make decisions every day about economic priorities as they spend or borrow money. However, they do not make them collectively and there is great inequality in who influences the direction of economic expenditure. There is no reason why the 'hidden hand' of the market should be seen as more rational than conscious deliberations about overall priorities in the allocation of economic capacity through money issue.

no, but very think? gut-feel

Democratic control of money creation would enable change and flexibility based on social and public priorities within the economy. This flexibility could create a steady state provisioning system through a careful linking of monetary and fiscal policies. As Galbraith has pointed out, fiscal policy can be used to manage excess demand as well as falling demand (1975:306–7). Tax could be used to regulate activities such as resource use, to redistribute wealth or to regulate money supply if it got out of hand. The importance of a steady state money system is that money issue would be determined by popular demand in the same way that private demand creates money now. If much of the money issued went directly to public provisioning as investment income for goods and service providers, or to individuals as a basic income, it would be hard for a state to divert this money to less appropriate expenditure such as armaments or warfare.

I wouldn't trust that!

What wd. Cecil Collins Fool say or do?

The main source of income for any remaining profit-based companies would be contracts from the public or communal sectors or the provision of goods and services to those sectors. This is the basis on which many commercial companies already operate. This would, arguably, provide a much more secure source of income than the ebb and flow of the market sector. As Minsky argued, government spending is more sustainable for the private sector because it is based on income rather than debt (Wray 2009:9). To have the money system driven from democratically controlled priorities would completely turn around the present economic drivers. It would not be the search for profit that would drive production, but social need and social priorities. Commercial firms would need to orient themselves to those priorities if they wished to apply for contracts. They would, however, still need credit to start the production process. This could come from the public sector as a prepayment for the contract or service. It could come from long term private investment, preferably as equity. Shares could be traded, but they would be subject to taxation and would have to be held for a period of time between buying and selling. Speculative investments that did not involve the direct production of goods and services for public benefit would be treated as gambling and taxed heavily, or even be proscribed. No private investments would be publicly guaranteed.

Given the way that the money creation system has been abused for private gain there is also a very strong case for a windfall tax on money wealth. Those people who have amassed huge incomes from manipulating money should be seen as profiteers and treated accordingly. *or aberrant ? 1u?*

Banking the People's Money

What emerges from the analysis of money and banking presented in this book is that modern banking is an act of money creation which the state must guarantee if the savings of the public are to be secured. Debt-driven money issue through the banking system also drives economic growth which is not sustainable in economic or ecological terms. The present banking system is therefore undemocratic and unsustainable. The public has the responsibility for the security of the banking system, but does not gain the benefit. Two of the mainstream solutions to the financial crisis are better regulation and the separation of high street savings from speculative finance. The first aims to regulate high street banks more strictly. The second would instigate 'narrow banking', separating off traditional banking services (Strange 1998:174). These solutions are linked. Regulation is about imposing rules on banks where public savings are at risk. Whether the banks are formally separated or not, it is argued that there must be firewalls between speculative activities and high street banking services. However, as long as both aspects of banking remain within the commercial sector, these solutions will fail as they have done in the past. It has proved impossible to separate the two sides of commercial banking. The end result has been that the public has had to back both the high street and the speculative aspects of capitalist finance.

As described in Chapter 3, the financialisation of the banking system has led people to confuse savings with capital and this has been largely a result of how the banks have been seen to operate. The assumption is that banks take in personal deposits and invest them for profit. Even if this were the case, such a model of banking is no longer practicable as there are insufficient bank deposits to provide enough liquidity to sustain profit (Langley 2010). Traditional 'narrow' banks also did not provide a broad-based public service because they were exclusionary in not offering services to the poor. The way that current banking is structured means that taking deposits enables money creation which, as we have seen, becomes a liability of the state. This creates unlimited 'moral hazard' as risky behaviour will always be underpinned by public rescue. The only safe way to separate high street banking from risk and speculation is to have no commercial involvement in the delivery of public banking services.

One of the mainstream solutions put forward has been to create smaller commercial banks that could be allowed to fail. This is the wrong argument. Banking that involves the creation of money should not be constructed on a commercial basis, therefore there is no case for failure. Public banking should be run on a not-for-profit basis through organisations such as the post office or on a mutual basis as the old building societies and savings banks did. Banks offering services to the public could be municipal, national, regional or based on specific sectors such as housing or agriculture. All of these types of organisations already exist, or have existed in the past. They would provide secure savings, safe lending and money transfer services. As not-for-profit organisations would not have to pay dividends to shareholders, there would be no incentive to expand activities beyond what is necessary for sustainable provisioning. If the aim was to achieve a steady state economy interest would not be paid on saving deposits, although they could be inflation-proofed through some kind of national savings scheme.

No profit-based financial organisations would be able to take in savings deposits. Any money invested in for-profit financial organisations would be clearly linked to loans or other assets and only repaid when sufficient money had been returned. Any banking system issuing loans based on deposits returnable on demand will always be an exercise in money creation. Given the abuse of money creation by the private sector, no organisation that is given the capacity to issue money should be run for private profit. Only not-for-profit organisations should be able to create loans under the supervision of a monetary authority. Joseph Huber and James Robertson argue that national governments could reclaim the issue of money from the privatised banking system very easily by simply declaring all electronic sight accounts as legal tender (1999:20). As with notes and coin, it would be illegal for anyone other than the state, or another organisation representing the public interest, to create new loan-based sight accounts. Such a move would only be acknowledging the status quo, as all bank sight accounts can be 'cashed' at any time and are, in practice, subject to state guarantee.

Not-for-profit banks as deposit taking institutions would be creating money through loans, but such loans would be for social benefit, determined by publicly determined priorities. From a steady state perspective it would be important that loans were made interest free wherever possible and where appropriate as money could be issued as debt-free grants. Ideally, new money should be spent into circulation on socially responsible and sustainable projects. One possibility is to set up a revolving loan, or reinvestment fund. There are many examples of this within the co-operative and community finance movement (Affleck and Mellor 2003).These are funds that are usually set up by grant and then issued as loans for social benefit or to develop social or co-operative enterprises. As loans are repaid new ones are made. The level of lending or grant issued could vary: for example, a bank in a poorer area could make a higher proportion of grants than loans. Publicly generated money could also be distributed through democratically-based specialist banks. These could be geographic (local, regional, national) or specialist (health, arts, environment, housing). Non-commercial banks are not immune from risky or illegal activity as the US savings and loans crisis and the failure of building societies in the UK shows. However, these organisations were operating within a wider speculative climate. In a steady state economy the wider climate would not be conducive to speculative activity.

A major problem in establishing a steady state economy and reclaiming money as a public resource would be the nature of the global financial system. Such a solution would be hard to implement in one country: the campaign would therefore need to be taken to the global level.

International Money

Central to the neo-liberal global financial system has been the free flow of money. As the Bretton Woods system unravelled, capitalist finance slipped the boundaries of national economies and spread its tentacles around the globe. National currencies subject to market forces proved a field day for speculators, while creating severe economic problems for the countries concerned. Globalised production was able to play off hard currencies against soft currencies to maximise profits. A 'hard' reserve currency country, like the US, was able to flood the world with dollars, drawing in goods and services from around the world. As Graham Turner argues, the financial collapse was largely caused by globalised production. As western capital moved offshore to cheap labour areas and production declined in the home economies, the classic problem of the failure to realise profit emerged. There was plenty of surplus value in the goods as they were re-imported for sale, but a limit to purchasing power. Neither the workforce in the producer countries nor the consumers in the old industrial countries had sufficient money to buy the products. This meant that countries like the US ran huge deficits while western consumers bridged the gap with debt. As the deficits and profits were recycled, the excess money got sucked into inflationary investment cycles including house price rises: 'the sharp rise in house prices was the logical outcome of Western companies aggressively cutting labour costs by shifting jobs abroad' (Turner 2008:61).

Rawi Abdelal reminds us that globalised production and the free movement of capital is relatively recent, largely stemming from the 1980s (2007:213). He argues that globalised finance as an orthodoxy peaked in the late 1990s and the case for reform is being discussed in many quarters. As he points out, 'the globalization of finance is neither inexorable nor inevitable'; however, while people accept the orthodoxy 'we may not recognise the inherent fragility of the underpinnings of a world that allows such extraordinary mobility of capital' (Abdelal 2007:223). Democratic control of currency and banking can only take place within a sphere of public authority. In the absence of a global democratic forum the most immediately feasible level is the nation state, although for green economists it would be better to align money systems with ecological systems such as bioregions (Scott Cato 2009 150–151). Whatever the level, any decisions made locally will be overwhelmed if currencies cannot be insulated from each other. Global inequality will also persist if currencies such as the dollar or the euro continue to dominate. Jane D'Arista suggests that one way around this problem would be to enable all countries to make transnational payments in their own currency (2004:202). This would remove the need for countries to earn money from a stronger currency before being able to trade internationally, but it would not remove the opportunity to speculate between currencies. Nor would it eliminate the inequalities between countries.

Another solution would be to put a barrier between national currencies, that is, to have a currency of account at the global level. The answer that Keynes proposed was a global money system. Keynes warned that free trade, flexible exchange rates and free movement of capital was incompatible with maintaining full employment. Keynes wanted countries to interact via a buffer mechanism, the *bancor* (bank gold) (Scott Cato 2009:77). This would be a flexible international payments system which would also have a mechanism to balance world trade whereby surplus economies would compensate debtor economies. This part of the Bretton Woods discussion was never implemented, instead there was a gold exchange rate mechanism based around the dollar.

Huber and Robertson call for an international currency issued by an independent international authority. This would be given to the UN to spend into circulation to help finance its own operations, but could also be given proportionately to national governments as a redistributive measure, a form of international 'basic income' (2000:56). Bernard Lietaer advocates a global currency linked to land (2001:249) while Richard Douthwaite suggests it should be an EBCU, an energy-backed currency unit (1999:57). More recently, Davidson has argued for an International Monetary Clearing Unit (IMCU) which would insulate economies from each other (Davidson 2008:300–305). Only central banks would be able to access the units and exchange them with other central banks. This means that currencies could be insulated from each other, eliminating the opportunity for currency speculation and the inequality created by 'hard' and 'soft' currencies. It would also enable governments to monitor payments for illegal activities or tax evasion. Another possibility that would help remove the inequalities between countries would be to value a global currency on some equivalent to average income so that there would be parity in relation to labour costs. This would remove the benefit of production in low wage countries and encourage production at the point of use.

Conclusion

The most important lesson from the crisis of capitalist finance is that there *is* an alternative (Mellor 2006). Many of the ideas set out above are feasible and sensible. Key elements already exist. Money is a public resource and a public responsibility that has been harnessed for private profit. The public nature of money has been clearly demonstrated in the financial crisis. The total irresponsibility and blatant incompetence of speculative capitalism has also been revealed, as well as its fragility. Capitalist finance has proved itself to be an unworthy steward of national wealth. It has abused and dissipated it. Contrary to capitalist propaganda, money is not made by wealth creators in the private sector. It is created through the banking system and then expropriated by a minority for private profit. There is no justification for allowing the benefits arising from the creation of a country's money supply to be appropriated by greed and self-interest. If money is ultimately the responsibility of the public, its ownership and control should be given back to the public. Money is a public resource that should be used to provision human societies on the basis of social justice, well-being and environmental responsibility. A steady state economy would be possible if the money system was not driven by the demands of debt-based money, financial accumulation and profit-driven growth. Money should be reclaimed and democratised for the benefit of the whole of society and the natural world. It is the people's money: give it back to the people.

APPENDIX:
ACRONYMS AND ABBREVIATIONS

ABS	Asset-Based Securities
BIS	Bank for International Settlements
CDOs	Collatoralised Debt Obligations
CDS	Credit Default Swaps
EBCU	Energy-Backed Currency Unit
FSA	Financial Services Authority
GDP	Gross Domestic Product
HBoS	Halifax Bank of Scotland
IMF	International Monetary Fund
LETS	Local Exchange Trading Systems
LIBOR	London Interbank Offered Rate
LTCM	Long Term Capital Management
MBS	Mortgage Backed Securities
NINJA	No Income, No Job, No Assets
OECD	Organisation for Economic Co-operation and Development
PFI	Private Finance Initiative
SARS	Suspicious Activity Reports
SIVs	Structured Investment Vehicles
TARP	Troubled Asset Relief Programme

BIBLIOGRAPHY

Abdelal, Rawi (2007) *Capital Rules: The Construction of Global Finance* Harvard University Press, Cambridge MA

Affleck, Arthur and Mary Mellor (2003) *Social Investment in the North East of England* Sustainable Cities Research Institute, Northumbria University

— (2006) 'Community Development Finance: A neo-market solution to social exclusion?', *Journal of Social Policy*, Vol. 35, No. 2, pp.303–19

Albert, Michael (2003) *Parecon: Life after capitalism* Verso, London

Baran, Paul A. and Sweezy, Paul M. (1966) *Monopoly Capital* Monthly Review Press, New York

Bennholdt-Thomsen Veronika and Maria Mies (1999) *The Subsistence Perspective* Zed Press, London

Bennholdt-Thomsen Veronika, Nicholas Faraclas and Claudia von Werlhof (eds) (2001) *There is an alternative: Subsistence and worldwide resistance to corporate globalization* Zed Press, London

Black, William Kurt (2008) 'Why Greenspan's and Bush's Regulatory Failures Allowed a 'Criminogenic Environment' *Report of 17th Annual Hyman Minsky Conference*, 17–18 April, New York, available at www.levy.org (last accessed April 2009)

Blackburn, Robin (2006) *Age Shock* Verso, London

— (2008) 'The Subprime Crisis', *New Left Review*, Vol. 50, pp.63–108

Blain, Bob (1987) 'United States Public and Private Debt 1791–2000', *UNESCO International Social Science Journal*, pp.577–91, available at www.siue.edu/~rblain/usdebt.htm (last accessed July 2008)

Boaventura de Sousa, Santos (ed.) (2006) *Another Production is Possible* Verso, London

Brenner, Robert (2002) *The Boom and the Bubble: The US in the World Economy* Verso, London

Brittain-Catlin, William (2006) *Offshore: The Dark Side of the Global Economy* Picador, London

Brummer, Alex (2008) *The Crunch: The Scandal of Northern Rock and the Escalating Credit Crisis* Random House, London

Bryan, Dick and Mike Rafferty (2007) 'Financial Derivatives: Bubble or Anchor', in Libby Assassi, Anastasia Nesvetailove and Duncan Wigan (eds) *Global Finance in the New Century* Palgrave Macmillan, Basingstoke

Buchan, James (1997) *Frozen Desire* Picador, London

Buiter, Willem (2007) 'Lessons from the 2007 Financial Crisis' Centre for Economic Policy Research Discussion. Paper No. DP6596, available at SSRN: http//ssrn.com/abstract=1140525 (last accessed August 2009)

— (2009a) http://blogs.ft.com/maverecon/2009/07/how-not-to-form-financial-markets (last accessed August 2009)

— (2009b) http://blogs.ft.com/maverecon (last accessed June 2009)

— (2009c) http://blogs.ft.com/maverecon/2009/07/how-not-to-form-financial-markets (last accessed August 2009)

Burrough, Bryan and John Helyar (1990) *The Barbarians at the Gate* Harper Row, New York

Bush, Janet (2006) 'Sell-out: Why hedge funds will destroy the world', *New Statesman*, 31 July, pp.26–9

Cable, Vince (2009) *The Storm: The World Economic Crisis and What it Means* Atlantic Books, London

Chick, Victoria (1992) *On Money, Method and Keynes* Macmillan, Basingstoke

— (2000) 'Money and Effective Demand', in John Smithin (ed.) *What is Money?* Routledge, London

CNNMoney (2009) www.CNNMoney.com (last accessed June 2009)

Collard, S. and E. Kempson (2005) *Affordable Credit: The Way Forward* Joseph Rowntree Foundation/The Policy Press, Bristol

D'Arista, Jane (2003) 'Financial Architecture in the 21st Century?', in Ann Pettifor (ed.) *Real World Economic Outlook* Palgrave Macmillan, Basingstoke

— (2008) 'Broken Systems: Agendas for Financial and Monetary Reform', *Report of 17th Annual Hyman Minsky Conference*, 17–18 April, New York, available at www.levy.org (last accessed April 2009)

Daly, Hermann (ed.) (1973) *Towards a Steady State Economy* W.H. Freeman, San Francisco

— (1999) *Ecological Economics and the Ecology of Economics* Edward Elgar, Cheltenham

Davidson, Paul (2008) 'Reforming the World's International Money', *Real-World Economics Review*, No. 48, pp.306–11, available at www.paecon.net/PAEReview/issue48/Davidson48.pdf (last accessed July 2009)

Davies, Glynn (2002) *A History of Money* University of Wales Press, Cardiff

De Goede, Marieke (2005) *Virtue, Fortune and Faith* University of Minnesota Press, Minneapolis

De Soto, Hernando (2000) *The Mystery of Capital* Bantam Press, London

Dodd, Nigel (1994) *The Sociology of Money* Polity, Cambridge

Douthwaite, Richard (1999) *The Ecology of Money* Green Books, Totnes

— (2000) *The Growth Illusion* Lilliput Press, Dublin

Douthwaite, Richard and Danial Wagman (1999) *Barataria: A community exchange network for the third system* Strohalm, Utrecht

Dymski, Gary (2007) 'From Financial Exploitation to Global Banking Instability: Two Overlooked Roots of the Subprime Crisis', available at www.soas.ac.uk/economics/events/crisis/file43938.pdf (last accessed August 2009)

Elliott, Larry and Dan Atkinson (2008) *The Gods that Failed: How Blind Faith in Markets has Cost Us Our Future* Bodley Head, London

Epstein, Gerald A. (ed.) (2005) *Financialization and the World Economy* Edward Elgar, Cheltenham

Ferguson, Naill (2002) *The Cash Nexus* Penguin, London

— (2008) *The Ascent of Money* Allen Lane, London

Fernando, Jude L. (2006) *Microfinance: Perils and Prospects* Routledge, Abingdon

Fisher, Thomas and M.S. Sriram (2002) *Beyond micro-credit: Putting development back into micro-finance* Oxfam/New Economics Foundation/Vistaar, London and Delhi

Foster, John Bellamy and Fred Magdoff (2009) *The Great Financial Crisis: Causes and Consequences* Monthly Review Press, New York

Franks, Thomas (2001) *One Market under God* Secker and Warburg, London

Freeland, Chrystia (2000) *Sale of the Century* Little Brown, London

Froud, J., Johal, S., Haslam, C. and K. Williams (2001) 'Accumulation Under Conditions of Inequality', *Review of International Political Economy*, Vol. 8, No. 1, pp.66–95

Fuller, Duncan and Mary Mellor (2008) 'Banking on the Poor: Advancing Financial Inclusion in Newcastle upon Tyne UK', *Urban Studies*, Vol. 45, No. 7, pp.1505–24

Galbraith, John Kenneth (1975) *Money: Whence it came and Where it went* Penguin, London

Georgescu-Roegen, Nicholas (1971) *The Entropy Law and the Economic Process* Harvard University Press, Cambridge, MA

Gibson-Graham, J.K. (1996) *The End of Capitalism (As We Knew It): A Feminist Critique of Political Economy* Oxford, Blackwell

Glyn, Andrew (2007) *Capitalism Unleashed: Finance, Globalisation and Welfare* Oxford University Press, Oxford

Gowan, Peter (2009) 'Crisis in the Heartland', *New Left Review*, Vol. 55, pp.5–30

Graziani, A. (2003) *The Monetary Circuit of Production* Cambridge University Press, Cambridge

Greenspan, Alan (2008) *The Age of Turbulence* Penguin, London

Harmer, Mercy (1999) 'A Green Look at Money', in Molly Scott Cato and Miriam Kennet (eds) *Green Economics* Green Audit, Aberystwyth

Harvey, David (1982) *The Limits to Capital* Blackwell, Oxford

— (2003) *The New Imperialism* Oxford University Press, Oxford

Henderson, Hazel (1981) *The Politics of the Solar Age: Alternatives to Economics* Anchor Press, Doubleday, New York

Hilferding, Rudolf (1910/1985) *Finance Capital* Routledge and Kegan Paul, London

Hillinger, Claude (2008) 'How to deal with the US financial crisis at no cost to the taxpayer', *Real-World Economics Review*, No. 48, pp.306–11, available at www.paecon.net/PAEReview/issue48/Hillinger48.pdf (last accessed May 2009)

Huber, Joseph and James Robertson (2000) *Creating New Money* New Economics Foundation, London

Hutchinson, Francis, Mellor, Mary and Wendy Olsen (2002) *The Politics of Money: Towards Sustainability and Economic Democracy* Pluto Press, London

Ingham, Geoffrey (1984) *Capitalism Divided: The city and industry in British Social Development* Macmillan, Basingstoke

— (2004) *The Nature of Money* Polity, Cambridge

Innes, Mitchell A. (1913/2004) 'What is Money?', in L. Randall Wray (2004) *Credit and State Theories of Money: The contribution of A. Mitchell Innes* Edward Elgar, Cheltenham

— (1914/2004) 'The Credit Theory of Money', in L. Randall Wray (2004) *Credit and State Theories of Money: The contribution of A. Mitchell Innes* Edward Elgar, Cheltenham

Jackson, Tim (2009) *Prosperity without Growth?* Sustainable Development Commission, Earthscan, London

Kallis, Giorgos, Martinez-Alier, Joan and Richard Norgaard (2009) 'Paper assets, real debts: An ecological exploration of the global economic crisis', *Critical Perspectives on International Business*, Vol. 5, No.1–2, pp.14–25

Keen, Steve (2001) *Debunking Economics: The Naked Emperor of the Social Sciences* Pluto Press, London

Kindleberger, Charles (1996) *Manias, Panics and Crashes* 3rd edition, Macmillan, Basingstoke

Knapp, G.F. (1924) *The State Theory of Money* Macmillan, London

Krugman, Paul (2008) *The Return of Depression Economics* Penguin, London

Langley, Paul (2002) *World Financial Orders* Routledge, London

— (2006) 'The making of investor subjects in Anglo–American pensions', *Environment and Planning D: Society and Space* Vol. 24, No. 6, pp.919–34

— (2008) *The Everyday Life of Global Finance* Oxford University Press, Oxford

— (2010) 'The Performance of Liquidity in the Subprime Mortgage Crisis', *New Political Economy* (forthcoming)

Lapavitsas, Costas (2003) *Social Foundations of Markets, Money and Credit* Routledge, London

Lapavitsas, Costas and Saad-Filho, Alfredo (2000) 'The Supply of Credit Money and Capital Accumulation: A Critical view of post-Keysian analysis', in Paul Zarembka (ed.) *Value, Capitalist Dynamics and Money* Jai Elsevier Science, London

Large, Martin (2010) *Common Wealth for a free, equal, mutual and sustainable society* Hawthorn Press, Stroud

Lawson, Neal (2009) *All Consuming* Penguin, London

Lewis, Nathan (2007) *Gold: The once and future money* John Wiley and Sons, New Jersey

Leyshon, A. and N. Thrift (1997) *Money/Space: Geographies of monetary transformation* Routledge, London

Lietaer, Bernard (2001) *The Future of Money* Century, London

Lord, Clive (1999) 'An Introduction to Citizen's Income', in Molly Scott Cato and Miriam Kennet (eds) *Green Economics* Green Audit, Aberystwyth

Lowenstein, Roger (2001) *When Genius Failed: The Rise and Fall of Long-Term Capital Management* Fourth Estate, London

MacKenzie, Donald (2008) 'What's in a number? The importance of LIBOR', *Real-world economics review*, Issue No. 7, No. 43, pp.237–42

Margolis, Mac (2007) 'The Microcredit Backlash', *Newsweek*, 3 April

Martinez-Alier, Joan (1987) *Ecological Economics* Blackwell, Oxford

Marx, Karl (1867/1954) *Capital Vol I* Lawrence and Wishart, London

Mason, Paul (2009) *Meltdown* Verso, London

McCulley, Paul A. (2008) 'A Reverse Minsky Journey', *Report of 17th Annual Hyman Minsky Conference*, 17–18 April, New York, available at www.levy.org (last accessed April 2009)

Mellor, Mary (1997) 'Women, nature and the social construction of "economic man"', *Ecological Economics*, Vol. 20, No. 2, pp.129–40

— (2005) 'The Politics of Money and Credit as A Route To Ecological Sustainability and Economic Democracy', *Capitalism, Nature, Socialism*, Vol. 16, No. 2, pp.45–60

— (2006) 'Bringing economics down to earth: There is an Alternative', *Soundings*, No. 34, pp.22–32

— (2009) 'Ecofeminist Political Economy and the Politics of Money', in Ariel Salleh (ed.) *Eco-Sufficiency and Global Justice* Pluto Press, London

Mellor, Mary, Hannah, Janet and John Stirling (1988) *Worker Co-operatives in Theory and Practice* Open University Press, Milton Keynes

Merricks, Linda (1996) 'Frederick Soddy: Scientist, Economist and Environmentalist', *Capitalism Nature Socialism*, Vol. 7, No. 4, pp.59–78

Mies, Maria (1998) *Patriarchy and Accumulation on a World Scale* Zed Press, London

Mies, Maria and Vandana Shiva (1993) *Ecofeminism* Zed Press, London

Morris, Charles R. (2008) *The Two Trillian Dollar Meltdown* Public Affairs, New York

Murphy, Richard (2009) 'Tax justice and secrecy jurisdictions', *Soundings*, No. 41, April, pp.65–76

Nesvetailova, Anastasia (2007) *Fragile Finance: Debt, Speculation and Crisis in an Age of Global Credit* Palgrave Macmillan, Basingstoke

North, Peter (2007) *Money and Liberation*, University of Minnesota Press, Minneapolis

Nylen, William R. (2003) *Participatory Democracy versus Elitist Democracy: Lessons from Brazil* Palgrave Macmillan, New York

O'Connor, James (1996) 'The Second Contradiction of Capital', in Ted Benton (ed.) *The Greening of Marxism* Guilford Press, New York

Panitch, Leo and Martijn Konings (2009) 'Myths of Neoliberal Deregulation', *New Left Review*, Vol. 57, pp.67–83

Parenteau, Robert W. (2008) 'Financial Markets Meltdown: What Can We Learn from Minsky?' *Report of 17th Annual Hyman Minsky Conference*, 17–18 April, New York, available at www.levy.org (last accessed April 2009)

Parguez, Alain and Mario Seccareccia (2000) 'The credit theory of money: The money circuit approach', in John Smithin (ed.) *What is Money?* Routledge, London

Pearce, John (2003) *Social Enterprise in Anytown* Calouste Gulbenkian Foundation, London

Pearson, Ruth (2001) 'Continuity and Change', in Beverly Lemire, Ruth Pearson and Gail Campbell (eds) *Women and Credit* Berg, Oxford

Perelman, Michael (2003) *The Perverse Economy* Palgrave Macmillan, Basingstoke

Perkins, Ellie and Edith Kuiper (eds) (2005) 'Explorations: Feminist Ecological Economics', *Feminist Economics*, Vol. 11, No. 3, pp.107–48

Peston, Robert (2008) *Who Runs Britain: How the super rich are changing our lives* Hodder and Stoughton, London

Pettifor, Ann (ed.) (2003) *Real World Economic Outlook* Palgrave Macmillan, Basingstoke

— (2006) *The Coming First World Debt Crisis* Palgrave Macmillan, Basingstoke

Phillips, Kevin (2008) *Bad Money* Viking, New York

Polanyi, Karl (1944) *The Great Transformation* Beacon Press, Boston

Pollock, Allyson (2004) *NHS plc* Verso, London

Power, Marilyn (2004) 'Social provisioning as a starting point for feminist economics', *Feminist Economics*, Vol. 10, No. 3, pp.3–19

Pym, Hugh and Nick Kochan (2008) *What Happened?* Old Street Publishing, London

Raddon, Mary-Beth (2003) *Community and Money* Black Rose Books, Montreal

Robertson, James (1998) *Transforming Economic Life* Schumacher Society and New Economics Foundation, London

Robertson, James and John M. Bunzl (2003) *Monetary Reform: Making it Happen!* ISPO, London

Ronald, Richard (2008) *The Ideology of Home Ownership* Palgrave Macmillan, Basingstoke

Rossi, Sergio (2007) *Money and Payments in Theory and Practice* Routledge, London

Roubini, Nouriel (2006) 'Why Central Banks Should Bust Bubbles', *International Finance*, Vol. 9, No. 1, pp.87–107

Rowbotham, Michael (1998) *The Grip of Death: A study of modern money, debt slavery and destructive economics* Jon Carpenter Press, Charlbury

Saul, John Ralston (2005) *The Collapse of Globalism* Atlantic Books, London

Schumacher, E.F. (1973) *Small is Beautiful* Abacus, London

Scott Cato, Molly (2006) *Market Schmarket: Building the Post-Capitalist Economy* New Clarion Press, Cheltenham

— (2009) *Green Economics* Earthscan, London

Scurlock, James D. (2007) *Maxed Out: Hard Times, Easy Credit* Harper Collins, London

Simmel, Georg (1907/1970) *The Philosophy of Money*, edited by David Frisby (1990) Routledge, London

Smithin, John (2000) 'What is Money?', Introduction in John Smithin (ed.) *What is Money?* Routledge, London

— (2009) *Money, Enterprise and Income Distribution* Routledge, London

Soros, George (2008a) 'The Crisis and what to do about it', *Real-World Economics Review*, No. 48, pp.306–11, available at www.paecon.net/PAEReview/issue48/Soros48.pdf (last accessed April 2009)

— (2008b) *The New Paradigm for Financial Markets* Public Affairs, New York

Spufford, P. (1988) *Money and its Use in Medieval Europe* Cambridge University Press, Cambridge

Stanford, Jim (2008) *Economics for Everyone* Pluto Press, London

Strange, Susan (1986) *Casino Capitalism* Blackwell, London
— (1998) *Mad Money* Manchester University Press, Manchester
Stretton, Hugh (1999) *Economics* Pluto Press, London
Tett, Gillian (2009) *Fool's Gold* Little Brown, London
Tobin, J. (1963) 'Commercial Banks and Creators of Money', in D. Carson (ed.) *Banking and Monetary Studies* Unwin, Homewood, Illinois
Turner, Graham (2008) *The Credit Crunch* Pluto Press, London
Veblen, Thorstein (1899) *The Theory of the Leisure Class* Mentor Books, New York
Veneroso, Frank, (2008) 'Financial Crisis: Prospect of a Second Wave', *Report of 17th Annual Hyman Minsky Conference*, 17–18 April, New York, available at www.levy.org (last accessed April 2009)
Wade, Robert (2008) 'Financial Regime Change?', *New Left Review*, Vol. 53, pp.5– 22
Walters, Brian (2008) *The Fall of Northern Rock* Harriman House, Petersfield
Warburton, Peter (1999) *Debt and Delusion* Allen Lane, London
Wigan, D. (2009) 'Financialisation and Derivatives: Constructing an Artifice of Indifference', *Competition and Change*, Vol. 13, No. 2, pp.157–72
Wood, Ellen Meikins (1999) *The Origin of Capitalism* Monthly Review Press, New York
Woodin, Michael and Caroline Lucas (2004) *The Green Alternative to Globalisation* Pluto Press, London
Wray, L. Randall (2004) 'Conclusion: The Credit Money and State Money Approaches', in L. Randall Wray (ed.) *Credit and State Theories of Money: The contribution of A. Mitchell Innes* Edward Elgar, Cheltenham
— (2008) 'Financial Markets Meltdown: What Can We Learn from Minksy', *Report of 17th Annual Hyman Minsky Conference*, 17–18 April, New York, Levy Economics Institute Report, Vol. 18, No. 3, pp.6–7
— (2009) *The Return of Big Government Public Policy Brief No 99*, Levy Institute, Bard College, Annandale-on-Hudson, New York
Zelizer, Viviana (1994) *The Social Meaning of Money* Basic Books, New York

INDEX

Compiled by Sue Carlton